ARGENTINA

BY CYNTHIA KENNEDY HENZEL

Essential Library

An Imprint of Abdo Publishing
abdobooks.com

ABDOBOOKS.COM

Published by Abdo Publishing, a division of ABDO, PO Box 398166, Minneapolis, Minnesota 55439. Copyright © 2023 by Abdo Consulting Group, Inc. International copyrights reserved in all countries. No part of this book may be reproduced in any form without written permission from the publisher. Essential Library™ is a trademark and logo of Abdo Publishing.

Printed in the United States of America, North Mankato, Minnesota.
102022
012023

Cover Photos: Shutterstock Images (Argentina); Shevalier Art/Shutterstock Images (pattern)
Interior Photos: Studio New-Art/Shutterstock Images, 4–5; Thiago Santos/Shutterstock Images, 8; Shutterstock Images, 10, 14, 23, 27, 28, 30–31, 37, 47, 57, 63, 66–67, 96, 101; Eric Isselee/Shutterstock Images, 11; Andrey Zheludev/Shutterstock Images, 13; Filip Fuxa/Shutterstock Images, 16–17; Peter Hermes Furian/Shutterstock Images, 19 (Argentina); Web Tools/Shutterstock Images, 19 (globe); Mark Green/Shutterstock Images, 21; Eva Mont/Shutterstock Images, 24; Oleksii G./Shutterstock Images, 29; Sergio Shumoff/Shutterstock Images, 34; Anthony Cooper/Science Source, 35; Ondrej Prosicky/Shutterstock Images, 39; Carolina Jaramillo/Shutterstock Images, 40–41; Sasa Huzjak/Alamy, 43; Diego Rayaces/Shutterstock Images, 46; The Print Collector/Hulton Archive/Getty Images, 49; Pictorial Press Ltd./Alamy, 51; Gisele Freund/Science Source, 52; iStockphoto, 54–55; Natacha Pisarenko/AP Images, 61; Guillermo Spelucin R./Shutterstock Images, 62; David Cannon/Allsport/Hulton Archive/Getty Images, 65; Frederic Legrand - Comeo/Shutterstock Images, 68; Carol Smiljan/NurPhoto/Getty Images, 71; Grupo 44/Latin Content WO, 73; Daniel Garcia/AFP/Getty Images, 75; Gustavo Garello/AP Images, 77; Tomas Cuesta/AFP/Getty Images, 78–79; Simon Mayer/Shutterstock Images, 80; Nacho Boullosa/SOPA Images/Sipa USA/AP Images, 82; NASA, 85; Franco Fafasuli/Getty Images News/Getty Images, 88–89; Joel Reyero/Picture Alliance/dpa/AP Images, 92; Sebastian Lopez Brach/Getty Images News/Getty Images, 95; Natacha Pisarenko/AP Images, 97; Marcelo Endelli/Getty Images Sport/Getty Images, 99

Editor: Angela Lim
Series Designer: Maggie Villaume

Library of Congress Control Number: 2022940078

PUBLISHER'S CATALOGING-IN-PUBLICATION DATA

Names: Henzel, Cynthia Kennedy, author.
Title: Argentina / by Cynthia Kennedy Henzel
Description: Minneapolis, Minnesota: Abdo Publishing, 2023 | Series: Essential Library of Countries | Includes online resources and index.
Identifiers: ISBN 9781532199356 (lib. bdg.) | ISBN 9781098274559 (ebook)
Subjects: LCSH: Argentina--Juvenile literature. | South America--Juvenile literature. | Argentina--History--Juvenile literature. | Geography--Juvenile literature.
Classification: DDC 982--dc23

CONTENTS

CHAPTER ONE

A TOUR OF ARGENTINA

Tanya stretches as the airplane taxis into the Pistarini Airport in Buenos Aires, Argentina. Together with her mother and her younger brother, Colin, Tanya is going to tour some of Argentina's famous sites before visiting her Aunt Gloria and Uncle Juan on their cattle ranch. They started the day with an early morning flight from Los Angeles, California. Now it is after 10:00 p.m. Tanya is glad that Mom arranged a car from the hotel to meet them instead of having to wait for a taxi.

Tanya sits back and gazes out the window as they ride to their hotel in downtown Buenos Aires, an important port city and the capital of Argentina.

Plaza de Mayo is the oldest public square in Buenos Aires. Many of Argentina's government buildings are located around the square.

Tanya hears Colin's stomach grumble, but she doubts there will be anywhere open to eat this late. However, as the car enters the city, Tanya is surprised to see restaurants teeming with people. Her mother explains that people in Argentina commonly eat dinner starting at about 10:00 p.m. Still, the family decides to find a quick snack instead of eating a full meal before they go to bed. They have to get up early because they have a big day ahead of them.

A DAY IN BUENOS AIRES

The next morning, they eat a big breakfast of sausage and eggs followed by *bolas de fraile*, which are pastries that are filled with a sweet, gooey filling called dulce de leche. After eating their fill, Tanya and her family go to Recoleta, the most elegant of Buenos Aires's neighborhoods. They stroll by exclusive boutiques and then past the Palacio Duhau, a glamorous hotel built in the 1930s for Argentina's growing upper class. Before leaving the neighborhood, they visit Recoleta Cemetery. It is filled with thousands of above-ground tombs called mausoleums. Tanya strolls through the

> Argentina had more than seven million tourists in 2019.[1]

beautifully carved structures. They conclude their visit at the mausoleum of Eva Perón, who was the much-beloved first lady of Argentina from 1946 to 1952.

The family's next sightseeing stop is San Telmo, the oldest neighborhood in Buenos Aires and the site of the San Telmo Market. The market building was originally constructed in 1897 as a place to sell fruits and vegetables. Today, antique shops and small boutiques fill the San Telmo Market. On weekends, the market spills out onto the city streets and attracts thousands of visitors.

Colin is not excited about shopping until the family goes to a leather goods store. There, he sees an interesting item—three leather straps with a rock hanging from each of them. The straps are knotted together at the top. Colin learns the item is a bola, a throwing weapon that was first used by Indigenous people to hunt. They would throw the bola at the legs of an animal. The leather straps would entangle and trap the creature. Gauchos, Argentine cowboys, later used bolas for herding cattle.

The family visits one more Buenos Aires neighborhood: La Boca. This is one of the city's working-class neighborhoods. It is known for its brightly colored buildings. Local artist Benito Quinquela Martín began painting the buildings in La Boca in the 1960s. Other artists followed his example, and today, the brilliantly colored buildings are tourist attractions. La Boca is also known for its devotion to the homegrown soccer team, Boca Juniors.

ATENEO GRAND SPLENDID BOOKSTORE

The Ateneo Grand Splendid Bookstore, located in Buenos Aires, is considered by many to be the most beautiful bookstore in the world. Originally constructed in 1919 as a theater, the building was restored and became the largest bookstore in Latin America in 2000. The ceiling is covered in ornate frescoes. Below, thousands of books are tucked into balconies and private nooks. Argentina is a literary country with one of the highest number of bookstores per person in the world.

Historically, immigrants settled in the La Boca neighborhood. Many of the immigrants came from Italy, but other European immigrants also established themselves in the area.

At 9:30 p.m., the family goes to a *parrilla*, a restaurant that features Argentine barbecue. As they eat side dishes of potatoes and grilled vegetables, waiters come by offering different cuts of meat on long skewers fresh from the barbecue. For dessert, Tanya chooses ice cream with *crema de leche*.

PENGUINS AT PUERTO MADRYN

The next morning, Tanya and her family fly to Puerto Madryn. As they travel south along the coast, Tanya spots ships heading in and out of busy harbors. After two hours, they land at the port city.

Puerto Madryn was founded in 1865. Much of the European influence in Argentina comes from Spain and Italy. However, the port city was founded by Welsh settlers. In the early 1800s, many Welsh people felt that their culture was in danger of disappearing due to the heavy influence of English culture. Welsh immigrants began to leave Wales to protect their cultural identity. In 1865, a wave of Welsh settlers arrived in Patagonia, a region at the southern tip of South America. They opened Welsh language schools. Influence from Welsh culture can still be seen in Patagonia today, and many people in the region speak Welsh.

Owain, a Welsh-Argentine tour guide, leads the family onto a small bus that takes them toward a penguin colony on Punta Tombo. Colin and Tanya watch for wildlife during the bus ride. They spot a ground bird about the size of a roadrunner with a crest of feathers on its head. They scan their guidebook for a gray bird with black markings and identify the bird as a tinamou. Colin points out a small animal with the body of a deer and the head of a rabbit but with shorter, pointed ears. Owain tells them it is a hoofed rodent called a mara, which is related to guinea pigs.

TRADITION DAY

Tradition Day is celebrated annually in November in San Antonio de Areco. Gauchos from all over the country gather to celebrate their ranching culture by riding through the streets and displaying their horsemanship. The celebration includes the *jineteada gaucha*, which is similar to a North American rodeo. As in North America, the Argentine rodeo includes wild bronco riding, in which riders try to stay on an unbroken horse for an allotted amount of time. There is great pride in winning the event.

Puerto Madryn is known for its abundance of wildlife, including sea lions, which can be seen lounging on the shores.

Owain passes around empanadas, small crescent-shaped pies, for lunch. He explains that different parts of the country are known for different fillings. Empanadas from the Pampas region in central Argentina are generally filled with beef, whereas seafood empanadas are more common along the Patagonian coast. Tanya tries one with lamb and onions. It is delicious!

Finally, the bus pulls into a parking area. They follow Owain down a winding narrow path. First, Tanya spots the ocean, which is deep blue against the lighter blue sky. Then, she sees the penguins!

Seasons in the Southern Hemisphere are opposite to seasons in the Northern Hemisphere. It is September, the beginning of spring in the Southern Hemisphere, and the Magellanic penguins are arriving at their breeding grounds. The males had come in first to prepare the nests—they scoop out a hole in the ground and collect a few rocks—and now the females are arriving from the ocean. With thousands of penguins waddling about, it isn't easy for the birds to find their mates. The males stand tall near their nests, calling in loud

NATURAL EASTER EGGS

There are more than 45 species of tinamou in Central and South America.[2] These birds lay some of the most colorful eggs in the world. Depending on the species, tinamou eggs may be bright blue, green, or deep chocolate brown. Tinamou eggs are also the shiniest eggs in the world, appearing much glossier than chicken eggs. Some of the eggs are iridescent, making them appear to shimmer with color. Scientists are studying tinamou eggs to see if they can find an evolutionary advantage in having such brilliantly colored shells.

cries for their mates. Magellanic penguins mate for life. The females push and bump about, trying to find their partners.

Tanya and Colin walk among the birds, careful not to touch them. The penguins might become aggressive if they think their nests are in danger. The penguins seem so tame, but Tanya reminds herself that these are wild animals. Tanya takes penguin selfies and laughs as the birds waddle around her.

The family heads back for the drive down the coast to view sea lions. The bus parks, and they walk to a low bluff overlooking the deep-blue ocean. A group of sea lions suns below them, occasionally making honking sounds. Tanya sees a baby sea lion that is just hours old. Among the sea lions are four elephant seals. Elephant seals are huge—up to 20 feet (6 m) long and 8,800 pounds (3,990 kg).[3] A male inflates his trunk-like snout and bellows.

After the outside activities, the family is ready for *merienda*, an afternoon custom in Argentina. Since people eat dinner late at night, they have a snack and rest in the afternoon. The bus stops at a tiny restaurant. Tanya and her family eat cucumber sandwiches, empanadas, and cakes. They drink cups of black tea with honey and milk. Tanya decides that she likes the merienda custom.

More than 1.5 million penguins breed in Punto Tombo each year.[4]

It is late at night by the time the family arrives back at the hotel room. After such a long day, Tanya and Colin are ready to say goodnight. It will be a two-hour drive to Uncle Juan and Aunt Gloria's ranch in the morning. There, in the vast plains of

Magellanic penguins return to the same nesting site from which they hatched to breed.

the Pampas, they will ride horses. Then they will travel north together to see the rain forest with its famous waterfalls. Tanya hopes she will see a toucan.

FANTASTIC ARGENTINA

Argentina is a country with beautiful natural landscapes. It spans an area from the snowy peaks of the Andes in the west to the Atlantic coast in the east, and from the subtropical rain forests

Los Glaciares National Park is a popular tourist destination in Argentina. The park was established in 1937 to protect its landscape diversity.

in the north to glaciers in the south. Tourists can enjoy the outdoors by hiking and skiing in the mountains, going on glacier excursions, whale watching, and seeing the largest waterfall system in the world.

In addition to natural beauty, Argentina has a unique past that gives the people a cultural flair that is not found elsewhere in South America. Indigenous peoples have had significant impacts on Argentine culture, including being the creators of the popular drink yerba maté. Much of Argentine culture, including language and food, is connected to Spanish colonialism and Italian influences. However, other Europeans, such as the Welsh, have had strong influences in parts of the country.

People in Buenos Aires enjoy one of the biggest cities in Latin America. They enjoy local festivals and cheer on their favorite soccer teams. Outside of Buenos Aires, there are many fantastic sites where Argentines and tourists can enjoy the outdoors. From towering mountains and vast plains to cities bustling with history and activity, there is much to see and learn about in Argentina.

CHAPTER TWO

GEOGRAPHY

Covering 1,073,518 square miles (2,780,398 sq km), Argentina is the eighth-largest country in the world and the second-largest country in South America by total area.[1] Located in the southeastern part of South America, it is about one-third the size of the United States. Argentina is bordered on the west by Chile and on the north by Bolivia and Paraguay. Brazil and Uruguay make up part of the country's eastern border along with the Atlantic Ocean.

Argentina includes several islands. Among these is Isla de Los Estados at the southern tip of the country. The island famously served as the inspiration for Jules Verne's novel *The Lighthouse at the End of the World*. Argentina also claims the Malvinas Islands.

Llamas graze on grasses in the Pampas region of Argentina.

However, the United Kingdom also lays claim to these islands, which are also known as the Falkland Islands. A portion of Antarctica belongs to Argentina.

Argentina is divided into roughly four geographic regions. The Andes is the mountainous region along the western border. The North extends from the tropical northern part of the country to the drier grasslands farther south. The Pampas is located in the central part of Argentina between the Andes Mountains and the Atlantic Ocean. Patagonia is a cold, dry region that lies from south of the Pampas to the tip of South America.

The Argentine-Chilean border is the third-longest land border between countries in the world at 4,158 miles (6,691 km).[4]

THE ANDES

The Andes Mountains form the world's longest mountain chain, stretching 5,500 miles (8,850 km) from the tip of South America to the Caribbean Sea.[2] The mountains run along the entire western border of Argentina. The highest peak in Argentina is located in the western part of the country in the Andes Mountains. Mount Aconcagua rises 22,831 feet (6,959 m) above sea level.[3] It is the tallest mountain in the Southern and Western Hemispheres.

The Andes have a significant effect on the climate of Argentina. Winds blow in from the west, bringing humid air from the Pacific Ocean into Chile. However, much of the humidity is lost as

MAP OF
ARGENTINA

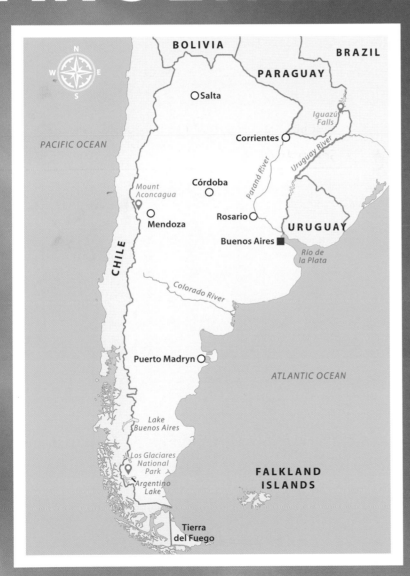

BOLIVIA
BRAZIL
PARAGUAY

N
W E
S

○ Salta

*Iguazú
Falls*

PACIFIC OCEAN

Corrientes ○

Paraná River

Uruguay River

*Mount
Aconcagua*

○ Córdoba

○ Mendoza

Rosario ○

URUGUAY

Buenos Aires ■

*Río de
la Plata*

Colorado River

CHILE

Puerto Madryn ○

ATLANTIC OCEAN

*Lake
Buenos Aires*

*Los Glaciares
National
Park*

*Argentino
Lake*

**FALKLAND
ISLANDS**

Tierra
del Fuego

KEY:
■ Capital
○ City
📍 Point of Interest

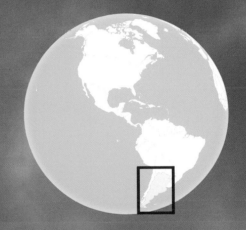

the air travels over the Andes Mountains into Argentina. The dry air warms as it travels down the Argentine slopes, making the western part of the country more arid than the eastern part.

Generally, temperatures in the Andes become cooler as the mountain range extends southward, farther from the equator. However, other variables such as elevation, wind, precipitation, and the direction that slopes face cause a lot of variation in the climate of the Andes. In addition to mountain peaks, the Andes have other geographical features. The region has glacial moraines and alpine lakes. The Andean Patagonian Forest covers a portion of the Andes Mountains and is the world's southernmost forest. The southern region of the Andes is marked by glaciers, ice fields, and high, flat areas of land called plateaus.

HOW THE ANDES FORMED

Tectonic plates are massive slabs of rock under the continents and oceans. The plates move slowly over time. Volcanoes and earthquakes often occur between plates as they move. The Andes Mountains are the result of the Nazca Plate being pushed under the South American Plate. The mountains get gradually taller as one plate pushes the other up. This activity continues today, causing earthquakes and volcanic eruptions.

Lake Buenos Aires lies high in the Andes on the border between Argentina and Chile. In Chile, the lake is called General Carrera Lake. It is part of the Lake District, a popular tourist destination that includes many of Argentina's scenic lakes. Lake Buenos Aires is the largest freshwater lake in Argentina. The deep turquoise waters cover 714 square miles (1,850 sq km), with 340 square miles (880 sq km) in Argentina.[5]

The Perito Moreno Glacier is approximately 19 miles (31 km) long.

Farther south, Argentino Lake receives water from the Perito Moreno Glacier. Perito Moreno is one of the few glaciers in the world that continues to grow despite global warming. The heavy snowfall in the region accounts for its growth. Argentino Lake is famous for a peculiar phenomenon. Ice from the Perito Moreno Glacier extends until it forms a natural dam across the lake. Lake water builds up behind the dam and begins to wear a tunnel through the thick ice. Approximately every two to four years, the tunnel collapses. Chunks of glacial ice crash into the lake and create spectacular waves.

Also located in the southern part of the Andes, Los Glaciares National Park protects about 2,807 square miles (7,270 sq km) of glaciers, lakes, plateaus, ice fields, and forests.[6] The park is home to Mount Fitz Roy. This ice and granite peak, which is often shrouded in clouds at the summit, is considered one of the most difficult ascents in the world by climbers.

THE NORTH

As the name suggests, the North is the geographic region in northern Argentina. It includes the Gran Chaco area in the west and Mesopotamia area in the east. The Gran Chaco extends into Bolivia, Brazil, and Paraguay, but two-thirds of its area is in Argentina. The foothills of the Andes form the western border of the Gran Chaco while the Paraguay and Paraná Rivers form the eastern boundary. The Gran Chaco contains the second-largest forest in South America, behind only the Amazon rain forest.

The Gran Chaco is hot and semiarid. Temperatures can reach 120 degrees Fahrenheit (49°C) in the summer.[7] Many of the rivers flowing east from the Andes dry up before reaching the Paraná River. The western part of the Gran Chaco has large, infertile salt flats. This area is prone to flooding during the summer as snow melts in the Andes Mountains. The Gran Chaco becomes more hospitable farther east, where temperatures are more moderate. Annual rainfall increases gradually from the west to the east.

Mesopotamia is another area in the North. It is located east of the Gran Chaco. *Mesopotamia* means "between the rivers," and the area is bounded by the Paraná River to the west and the Uruguay River to the east. The Uruguay River also forms the boundary between Argentina and the countries of Brazil and Uruguay. Both of these large rivers begin in Brazil and flow southward, joining the Río de la Plata and emptying into the Atlantic Ocean.

Mesopotamia is a long, narrow strip of land that is only 180 miles (290 km) across at its widest point.[8] The elevation of Mesopotamia decreases from north to south. Rainfall averages 80 inches (203 cm) per year.[9] Northern Mesopotamia has subtropical rain forests. Farther south, lowlands along the rivers are swampy and

The Salinas Grandes are the largest salt flats in Argentina.

23

The highest drop in the Iguazú Falls waterfall system is 262 feet (80 m).

densely forested. These swamps eventually give way to low grassy knolls.

The Iguazú Falls waterfall system is located in Mesopotamia on the border between Argentina and Brazil. *Iguazú* comes from Guaraní—an Indigenous language—and means "great water." The Iguazú Falls are the largest waterfall system in the world and include approximately 275 different waterfalls. Altogether, the waterfall system is 1.7 miles (2.7 km) wide.[10] Iguazú National Park, where the waterfall system is located, is a United Nations Educational, Scientific, and Cultural Organization (UNESCO) World Heritage site.

THE PAMPAS

The Pampas lie south of the North geographic region. The vast grassland covers approximately one-third of the country. *Pampas* comes from Quechua—a language spoken by many Indigenous nations in the Andes—and means "flat plains." The plains have fertile soil that makes the Pampas the agricultural center of the country. Buenos Aires lies in the eastern portion of the Pampas. Other major cities in the region include Córdoba and Mendoza.

As in the Gran Chaco, the average rainfall in the Pampas varies from west to east. The Dry Pampas in the west receive an average of 20 inches (51 cm) per year, whereas the Humid Pampas in the east get about 40 inches (102 cm) per year.[11] The Dry Pampas have short grasses that are suitable for grazing cattle. Taller, lusher grasses grow in the Humid Pampas, but most of the region has been plowed for agriculture.

In the central area of the Pampas is Mar Chiquita, a large salt lake. The lake has no outlet, so salts cannot wash out to other bodies of water. During the dry season, evaporation causes the salt in the water to become even more concentrated. Mar Chiquita is approximately 35 feet (11 m) deep and varies in size depending on the season. During the dry season, the lake shrinks to approximately 770 square miles (1,995 sq km), but during the rainy season it can swell to about 2,320 square miles (6,010 sq km).[12]

PATAGONIA

Patagonia lies south of the Pampas and extends to the southern tip of South America. The Colorado River forms the approximate northern boundary of Patagonia. Patagonia is a windswept plateau that primarily consists of steppe and desert. Port cities such as Comodoro Rivadavia and Santa Cruz are located in Patagonia.

The climate in Patagonia is heavily influenced by the Andes Mountains and ocean currents. In general, the region is cooler and drier than other regions of the country. Average temperatures throughout Patagonia range from 40 to 55 degrees Fahrenheit (4 to 13°C).[13] However, winds from

Some regions of Patagonia are known for clear skies that are perfect for stargazing.

the mountains and oceans can make temperatures feel even colder. The region typically receives less than 30 inches (76 cm) of rain each year.[14]

The Andes Mountains and the western edge of Patagonia sit on the Ring of Fire, a large range of volcanoes along the Pacific Ocean. Several volcanoes in Patagonia are considered active, including the Domuyo Volcano and Tromen. Elevation decreases from west to east. Laguna del Carbón, located near Argentina's Atlantic coast, is the lowest point in Argentina as well as the lowest point in the Southern and Western Hemispheres. It is 344 feet (105 m) below sea level.[15]

The Strait of Magellan lies at the tip of South America, connecting the Atlantic and Pacific Oceans. The strait separates South America from a chain of islands that forms the Tierra del Fuego archipelago. Grand Island is the largest island of the chain, but Tierra del Fuego is also made up of many smaller islands. About one-third of Grand Island belongs to Argentina, and the remainder belongs to Chile. Although the island chain is only about 620 miles (1,000 km) from Antarctica, temperatures rarely drop below freezing because of the effects of

DINOSAURS

Many dinosaur fossils have been found in Patagonia. Researchers have discovered remains of a species called *Mussaurus patagonicus*. The remains of these dinosaurs came from different life stages, suggesting that these dinosaurs lived together in herds. Another famous Argentine dinosaur is the *Argentinosaurus*, *pictured*, one of the largest land animals that ever lived. A fossilized femur indicates that the dinosaur may have been 131 feet (40 m) long and may have weighed about 110 tons (100 metric tons).[16]

The Andes Mountains extend into a portion of the Tierra del Fuego archipelago.

ocean currents.[17] The provincial capital city of Tierra del Fuego, Ushuaia, is the southernmost city in the world.

Argentina has a varied geography from the continent's highest mountains in the west to the coasts in the east. It has hot, arid areas as well as wet, tropical regions. Vast plains lie in central Argentina. The windswept landscapes of Patagonia lie to the south. This great diversity in geography creates great biodiversity and opportunities for tourism.

The Strait of Magellan runs for 350 miles (563 km).[18]

CHAPTER THREE

PLANTS AND ANIMALS

Argentina has a diverse range of plants and animals due to the country's array of landforms and climate. Wildlife varies depending on elevation as well as distance from the equator. Temperatures at high altitudes can be very cold, making it difficult for plants or animals to survive. In the southern Andes, forests consist of mostly conifer and oak trees. The Lake District has beech and myrtle forests. Forests in the North include tree species that are better adapted to the warm, arid climate.

Animals in the Andes include the vicuña, an animal that looks similar to an alpaca. It is the smallest species of the camel family. The smallest species of deer, the

Argentina is home to 14 wildcat species, including the jaguarundi.

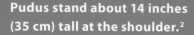

Pudus stand about 14 inches (35 cm) tall at the shoulder.[2]

pudu, also lives in the mountains. Long-tailed chinchillas live in rocky areas at high altitudes. They have long, thick fur that keeps them warm. For protection from cold and from predators, chinchillas live together in colonies and take shelter in underground dens. However, the Andean mountain cat also lives in those areas above the tree line and preys on chinchillas. Two species of guinea pigs live in the northwestern Andes. The spectacled bear, the only bear native to South America, also calls the northwestern Andes home.

The Andean flamingo—the world's tallest species of flamingo—lives at high elevations in the Andes, moving to lower elevations for warmth when the weather gets cold. They live in shallow wetlands. Their populations are declining due to habitat loss from agricultural expansion.

With a wingspan of more than ten feet (3 m), the Andean condor is among the world's largest flying birds.[1] The Andes Mountains can be very windy, and the Andean condor's large wings help the bird glide on air currents as it searches for carrion, or dead animals, to eat.

THE NORTH

Rivers in the North host piranhas as well as other fish species. Piranhas are omnivores, meaning they eat both plants and animals. Their diet includes aquatic plants and algae, but they will also eat fish and crustaceans. Many species of reptiles live in the North, including iguanas, caimans, swamp turtles, and boa constrictors.

The most arid areas in the western portion of the Gran Chaco are characterized by shrublands and cacti such as the prickly pear and barrel cactus. In more humid areas, the region consists of arid subtropical forest. Vegetation is unable to grow where salt flats have formed.

Farther east, the Gran Chaco has great forests of quebracho trees, tall evergreen trees with sparse foliage and thick, cork-like bark. Quebracho trees are commercially important because their hardwood produces tannin, a material used to make leather. The area is home to tapirs. These animals have a piglike body and a short trunk that can be used to grab food. The Gran Chaco also provides a habitat for capybaras. Capybaras are the world's largest rodent, growing up to 4.3 feet (1.3 m) long.[3]

Mesopotamia is famous for its natural beauty. There are stands of trees interspersed with grassy areas. Wax palms grow in the flood zones. Forests thrive along the rivers, and Paraná pines grow at higher elevations. Many birds, including toucans and hummingbirds, live in this region. The area is also home to wild cats such as jaguars and ocelots.

A toucan's long bill helps it reach fruit on branches that cannot support the bird's weight.

THE PAMPAS

Scrubland forests grow in the Dry Pampas in the west, and grasslands thrive in the Humid

Pampas in the east. Pampas grass can reach ten feet (3 m) tall and is native to the area.[5] The

ombu tree is the only plant to tower over the flat grasslands. Despite its name, the ombu tree is not a tree at all. It is a large bush that can grow up to 60 feet (18 m) high. Its trunk can have a circumference of 50 feet (15 m).[6] The ombu tree has many adaptations that help it survive. Its sap is poisonous, which prevents grazing animals from eating it. Additionally, the bush is resistant to locusts and other pests. Its smooth, spongy trunk helps the ombu tree store water, allowing the plant to weather grassland fires and periods of drought. The bush has a wide canopy of dark-green leaves and greenish-white flowers that develop into crimson berries. The ombu tree is valued for its shade in an area where few tall plant species grow.

Cattle and horses have replaced many native animal species of the Pampas. Ranchers hunted or drove out guanacos, which are related to llamas, because they competed with cattle for food. Small deer and the plains viscacha, a burrowing rodent that looks like a large guinea

The grasses of the Pampas provide food and habitat for many animals.

pig, live in the Pampas. Plains viscacha live in large systems of underground burrows and mark the entrances to their burrows with piles of sticks, stones, and other objects.

Rheas, large flightless birds related to the ostrich, were once common in the Pampas. Females deposit their eggs in a communal nest. The males incubate the nest, which may contain as many as 50 eggs, and care for the chicks. Rhea numbers have declined due to overhunting. Rhea eggs and meat were used by humans as food, and their skins were used for leather. Today, regulations protect the birds from hunting and commercial farming.

The red ovenbird is another bird that is common in the Pampas and can also be found in the North. It is the national bird of Argentina. The ovenbird is named for the nest it builds, which is shaped like a Dutch oven. The nest is made of clay and sticks and built in trees. The ovenbird has a distinctive song, a trill that sounds like *teach-er*. It is adaptable and will often move into urban settings.

PATAGONIA

Deciduous and coniferous forests line the western part of Patagonia in the foothills of the

ARGENTINA'S ARMADILLOS

Argentina is home to both the largest and smallest species of armadillo. The giant armadillo in the North can grow to 3.3 feet (1 m) in length.[7] It has hinged bands of brown armor and up to 100 teeth, more than any other land mammal. It feeds primarily on termites and ants. In contrast, the pink fairy armadillo of the Pampas grows to be only 4.5 inches (11.4 cm) long.[8] It has white claws and pink armor with silky hair. Both species are threatened by habitat loss. Pink fairy armadillos also suffer because pesticides stick to the insects they eat.

Each southern right whale has a unique pattern of white markings on its face.

Andes Mountains. Arid scrublands make up most of Patagonia, featuring vegetation that can survive with little precipitation. Areas of Patagonia that receive more rainfall have grasslands.

The cold waters of the South Atlantic are home to many marine animals. Elephant seals, sea lions, dolphins, and fur seals live along the coast. Southern right whales migrate to the area near Puerto Madryn and the Valdés Peninsula from July to September to give birth. They are black with raised patches of white skin on their heads. Right whales do not have teeth. Instead, they have large plates of baleen, which are made of keratin. This tough, flexible material is also found in human fingernails. Right whales feed by taking in large mouthfuls of water. Then they close their mouths and push the water out of their mouths through the baleen plates. The plates keep small creatures such as zooplankton and krill from escaping. The whales then swallow the food.

Until 1935, right whales were widely hunted by whalers. Right whales were sources of oil, meat, and baleen. Baleen was used for making many products, including corsets, whips, and umbrella parts. Hunting southern right whales was made illegal in 1935, but the whales still face threats today. Industrialization along coasts, commercial fishing, and changes in water conditions due to climate change threaten the endangered southern right whales.

> **Southern right whales may grow to 56 feet (17 m).[11]**

Marine birds also make their homes along the coast. Southern rockhopper penguins live in southern Patagonia. They are among the smallest of penguin species, only 20 inches (51 cm) tall.[9] They are easily identified by the crest of yellow and black feathers on their heads, as well as their red eyes, red-orange beaks, and pink feet. They get their name from how they move, hopping across the rocky shores instead of waddling like most penguins.

There are 84 species of land mammals in Patagonia, with just over half of them being rodents.[10] Rodents like tuco-tucos, which look like stocky gophers with long tails, create burrows and live in

CORMORANTS

Four species of cormorants live in Patagonia. These large sea birds have hooked bills that help them eat fish and other sea creatures. Each of the four species has a different hunting style. The neotropic cormorant dives for fish from just a few feet above the water. The imperial cormorant feeds offshore, plunging as deep as 150 feet (46 m) underwater to catch fish near the seafloor.[12] The rock shag, or Magellanic cormorant, *pictured*, feeds close to shore on small fish and crustaceans. The red-legged cormorant hunts in cold, shallow waters, sitting on the surface of the water before diving below.

large colonies. There are also large mammals such as the guanaco. Predators in Patagonia include foxes, skunks, and several species of wildcats, such as Geoffroy's cat, a brown feline with black spots that is about the size of a house cat.

Vegetation in Tierra del Fuego is sparse, with small patches of bunch grass. The central part of the island is forested. The southern tip of Argentina is home to many types of wildlife. Birds such as the albatross and Magellanic woodpecker are common in Tierra del Fuego. The culpeo, or Fuegian fox, also lives in this region along with huillín, an endangered type of river otter.

Argentina is a large country that boasts environmental diversity. It is home to many plant and animal species, some that thrive high in the mountains and others that live in the ocean waters. Some of these creatures have become endangered due to human activity, but hunting regulations and environmental policies have helped some species to recover.

CHAPTER FOUR

HISTORY

The first people in what is present-day Argentina arrived between 15,000 and 18,000 years ago. In the Pampas, archaeologists have found stone tools that were used around 14,000 years ago to hunt more than 40 different types of animals, including extinct species such as the giant ground sloth. Some researchers believe these people settled in the region after crossing the Bering Strait—which separates Asia and North America—and taking boats along the Pacific coast.

The first permanent settlements in Argentina were built approximately 8,000 years ago. Many nations established themselves throughout the region, and each developed a different lifestyle depending on

The National Museum of the Cabildo in Buenos Aires houses artifacts from colonial Argentina to the early days of the country's independence.

where they lived. The Calchaquí people lived in northwestern Argentina. They cultivated crops on terraced fields and kept herds of llamas. The Calchaquí also wove textiles from llama hair and made ceramics. The Guaraní people lived farther east along the Paraguay River. They practiced slash-and-burn agriculture, clearing areas by cutting forests and burning vegetation to plant corn, cassava, and sweet potatoes. Some Guaraní people still live in Argentina today. The Araucanians, which later became the Mapuche Nation, lived in the western part of the Pampas and grew corn, beans, squash, potatoes, and peppers. They raised guinea pigs for meat and llamas for wool. In the years before Spanish colonizers arrived, the Argentina region had a population of approximately 300,000 people.[1] Members of Mapuche Nation still live in Argentina today.

ARRIVAL OF THE SPANISH

In the 1500s, the Spanish and the Portuguese competed to settle South America, despite the Indigenous nations already present on the continent. The Europeans believed the land was rich in silver and other resources. After conquering Peru, the Spanish traveled overland into the Argentina region. In 1536, Pedro de Mendoza founded the first Spanish settlement in the area, Santa María del Buen Aire, where present-day Buenos Aires is located. However, this settlement failed shortly afterward because of attacks by Indigenous people in the area and a lack of food.

The Spanish established Santiago del Estero in northwestern Argentina in 1553. It has been populated ever since and is the oldest continuously inhabited settlement in Argentina today. Spanish settlements in the northwestern region of Argentina were important for agriculture

Folk dancers perform in Santiago del Estero, where the first Spanish settlement was founded in the 1550s.

and trade. The location allowed the Spanish to trade for products in exchange for the silver that was being produced in Spanish mines in Peru. Other Spanish settlements were founded in the late 1500s, including Mendoza and Córdoba. Buenos Aires was reestablished in 1580.

The Spanish colonies adopted the *encomienda* system. The system gave Spanish officials control of the land as well as the Indigenous people living in the area. It required Indigenous people to pay tribute to the Spanish in the form of gold and labor. The Spanish were meant to protect and educate the Indigenous people, but many officials abused their power. They demanded large amounts of gold and forced the Indigenous people to work for many hours.

The Spanish used the encomienda system to enslave Indigenous people. Indigenous nations rebelled against the Spanish system. The Spanish responded with military force, and many Indigenous people fled Argentina after the failed rebellions.

In addition, the Spanish created a system of racial hierarchy called the *casta* system. The casta system placed people born in Europe at the highest rank. Creoles, people of Spanish descent who were born in the Americas, were second in status. Mixed-race individuals and Indigenous people were lower in social standing. The casta system was used to impose Spanish ideologies and cultures on the Indigenous people. The Spanish forced Indigenous people to convert to Catholicism, learn Spanish, and give up their own cultures.

In the 1600s and 1700s, Jesuit priests established themselves in northeastern Argentina. Jesuit priests belong to an order of Roman Catholicism. In Argentina, they worked to convert the Guaraní people to Catholicism. In general, the Jesuits had peaceful relations with the Indigenous people and encouraged the Guaraní to continue speaking their language. Jesuits also protected the

THE CALCHAQUÍ WARS

Many Indigenous nations resisted Spanish expansion and the encomienda system. The Calchaquí Wars marked a long period of conflict between the Spanish and the Diaguita Confederation, which includes the Calchaquí. Beginning in the 1560s, members of the Diaguita Confederation attacked the Spanish to protect their homelands and cultures. Major rebellions occurred in 1630 and again in 1660. However, the Spanish stopped the rebellions both times. They forced members of the Diaguita Confederation to work under the encomienda system or relocated them to other parts of South America.

Guaraní from Portuguese slavers who were also on the South American continent.

The Spanish and Portuguese fought over land ownership in Brazil and the Río de la Plata region. In 1750, both countries signed the Treaty of Madrid, which determined how land would be divided in South America. The treaty was widely unpopular

By the early 1700s, the Jesuit missions controlled an area the size of California with 100,000 Indigenous people.[2]

in both countries. As part of the Treaty of Madrid, Portugal gave control of the port city Colonia near Buenos Aires to Spain in exchange for territory where seven Jesuit missions were located. The Jesuits and the more than 30,000 Guaraní present on those missions would need to relocate to Spanish territory. The Jesuits did not want to leave their missions, and the Guaraní did not want to abandon their homelands. As the Jesuits and the Guaraní resisted the treaty, Spanish and Portuguese forces entered the region. They killed many Jesuits and Guaraní people, and the missions were destroyed in 1767. The Spanish captured and enslaved the surviving Guaraní people.

INDEPENDENCE

Spanish territories in South America were split into districts called viceroyalties. They were governed by officials called viceroys. The Viceroyalty of the Río de la Plata was created in 1776 and included present-day Argentina, Uruguay, Paraguay, and Bolivia. Its government was established in Buenos Aires.

The Jesuit mission at San Ignacio Miní was built in the 1600s. Its architecture is a blend of Spanish and Guaraní styles.

In the 1800s, France and Britain were at war overseas. Spain was allied with France, and the British overpowered the Spanish navy in 1805. With Spain occupied with the war, the British saw an opportunity to push Spain out of Argentina. The British invaded Buenos Aires in 1806 and again in 1807. The invasions failed, but they caused the Spanish viceroy to flee Buenos Aires both times. Because the viceroy fled, the creoles in the viceroyalty were forced to fend for themselves. They were able to push back the British during both invasions.

The success of the creoles gave them confidence in their ability to govern themselves. They challenged Spanish rule for the first time. They exiled the Spanish viceroy and appointed a viceroy of their choice. Argentines formed their first independent government, the Primera Junta. The Revolution of Buenos Aries on May 25, 1810, launched the war for independence.

Argentines declared their independence from Spain in the town of San Miguel de Tucumán in 1816.

On July 9, 1816, Argentina declared its independence from Spain as the United Provinces of the Río de la Plata. Years of fighting followed. The Argentines defeated Spain in the North. General José de San Martín and Simón Bolívar liberated Peru, eliminating the threat of Europeans invading from north of Argentina.

In 1825, the British officially recognized Argentina's independence from Spain. However, fighting continued on Argentine soil as authoritarian leaders with personal armies fought to keep control of their own regions. Official boundaries in South America were still not established by 1864. That year, the War of the Triple Alliance (1864–1870) broke out. Paraguay fought against

Argentina, Brazil, and Uruguay. The president of Paraguay wanted to establish an Atlantic port city for the country. The six-year war included some of the bloodiest battles in South American history. Once Paraguay was defeated, Argentina was the first of the allies to recover, which led to unification efforts in the country. Argentina was finally unified in 1880 and quickly became the wealthiest and most powerful country in South America.

THE GROWING YEARS

In the late 1870s, the Argentine government wanted to expand its control south of the Colorado River. There were many Indigenous people in this area who resisted Argentine expansion. In 1879, General Julio Argentino Roca led a campaign called the Conquest of the Desert with the goal of eliminating the Indigenous population from the Pampas and Patagonia. Roca and the military moved outward from Buenos Aires and began slaughtering every Indigenous person in their path. The Conquest of the Desert drastically reduced Indigenous

ARGENTINA'S BLACK POPULATION

In 1800, Black people made up approximately one-third of Argentina's population.[3] As in many colonies in the Americas, Europeans enslaved and transported Black people from Africa to work on farms and ranches. But in 2010, less than 1 percent of the Argentine population identified as Black.[4] There are several reasons for this. Black Argentines were forced to serve on the front lines of the War of the Triple Alliance, where they suffered heavy casualties. An epidemic of yellow fever also disproportionately affected Black Argentines. African cultures in Argentina also began to fade as Black people married people of other races.

populations throughout Argentina, forever changing Argentina's demographics. Today, the only areas in Argentina with a high number of Indigenous people are those that were untouched by Roca's campaign.

The Conquest of the Desert opened the Pampas for ranches and settlement by Europeans. People from Italy and Spain made up more than 80 percent of European immigrants, although there were also immigrants from France, Poland, Russia, Germany, and the United Kingdom.[5] As the market for food worldwide increased, the ranches modernized. Settlers brought in new breeds of cattle. They plowed under grasses of the Pampas and planted alfalfa to feed the cattle.

With the influx of immigrants, the country grew rapidly as manufacturing also expanded. Buenos Aires became the capital of Argentina in the 1880s. At this time, big ranchers and

In the late 1800s, Argentina's economy and influence boomed as it became a major exporter of agricultural goods.

49

businesspeople made up the majority of government officials. By 1908, Argentina had the seventh-highest per capita income in the world.[6]

ARGENTINA IN THE 1900s

Though Argentina's economy was strong in the early 1900s, the country's wealth was concentrated in the hands of the ruling class. The Radical Civic Union opposed the wealthy conservatives, but the political party had little success until 1912. That year, the Argentine Congress passed constitutional reforms that required all male citizens older than 18 to vote. With more eligible voters, Hipólito Irigoyen was elected as president in 1916. Irigoyen was a member of the Radical Civic Union and the first Argentine president who wasn't from the traditional ruling class.

From 1929 to 1939, the global economy suffered during a period known as the Great Depression. Unemployment rates skyrocketed, and consumer demand declined worldwide. The Argentine government, led by Irigoyen, protected the fortunes of the wealthy but did little to help the poor. Frustrated with government leadership, the Argentine military staged a coup and overthrew Irigoyen. Government rule remained unstable in Argentina for many years, with the military overthrowing civilian rulers during times of economic downturn.

In 1943, the military once again seized control of the government, which had been accused of election fraud. Colonel Juan Perón became the head of the National Department of Labor, where he began to build support from the working class. He gave paid holidays to industrial workers, improved working conditions, and supported unions.

Juan Perón, *center*, received a lot of support from Argentina's working class during his presidential term.

Perón was elected president in 1946. He nationalized the country's banks, having the government oversee them, and companies and began paying off Argentina's debt. Between 1946 and 1951, Argentine unions went from half a million to two million members.[7] However, Perón kept tight control as his administration handled communications between workers and companies.

Perón's wife, Eva, was a strong supporter of labor and women's suffrage. Perón put her in charge of labor relations. Eva—fondly called Evita by the Argentine people—was extremely popular and helped the country expanded health and welfare benefits.

Perón was widely popular during the first years of his presidency. The economy appeared to be growing, and laborers received more rights. In 1949, Perón called for a new constitution that would

EVITA

Eva Perón, also known as Evita, was born on May 7, 1919, in Los Toldos, Argentina. She was the child of Juan Duarte and Juana Ibarguren. The family was poor, and when Eva was 15 years old, she went to Buenos Aires to become an actor. There she met Juan Perón, and the two married in 1945. When her husband entered the presidential race, Eva became active in politics. She was a champion for the poor. After Perón was elected, Eva worked to guarantee wage increases. She began the Eva Perón Foundation, which established thousands of charitable institutions such as schools, hospitals, orphanages, and nursing homes.

Eva was diagnosed with cancer in 1950 and died two years later. Even in death, she was so powerful that political opponents stole her body and hid it in Italy. In 1971, the government of Argentina returned her remains to her husband while he was exiled in Madrid, Spain. After Perón's death, his third wife, Isabel, brought Eva's remains back to Argentina, and Eva was buried next to Perón in the presidential palace. Two years later, the body was moved again to the Duarte family crypt in Recoleta Cemetery, Buenos Aires. Eva Perón's life was the basis for the musical *Evita*, which was later adapted into a movie starring Madonna.

Eva Perón helped pass the 1947 law that granted Argentine women the right to vote.

allow him to be reelected for another term. He also limited his opposition by imprisoning political opponents and censoring the media. Perón won reelection in 1951. However, after Eva died in 1952, support for Perón declined. In addition, the economy began to struggle. Laborers went on strike, and the military intervened. By 1955, Perón had been ousted and forced into exile.

During the next years, Argentina became increasingly unstable as civilian and military regimes vied for power. General Alejandro Lanusse came into power in 1971. He encouraged the reformation of political parties, and his government invited Perón back into the country. In 1973, Perón was elected president for a third time. He insisted that his third wife, Isabel—whom the Argentines disliked—would serve as his vice president. Perón died the next year, unable to heal the political strife in Argentina.

FIVE PRESIDENTS IN TWO WEEKS

Argentina's political instability continued into the early 2000s. In the two-week period between December 20, 2001, and January 2, 2002, Argentina had five presidents. President Fernando de la Rúa resigned on December 20 amid an economic crisis. He was temporarily replaced by the head of the Senate, Ramón Puerta, while Congress chose a replacement. Congress chose Adolfo Rodríquez Saá as interim president. Saá resigned on December 31, and Eduardo Camaño was sworn in as interim president. Meanwhile, Congress worked to find a long-term solution. On January 2, Congress named Eduardo Duhalde as president. Duhalde remained president until 2003.

PEOPLE AND CULTURE

I n 2021, Argentina had a population of 45.8 million. More than 97 percent of Argentines have European ancestry. Argentina has a relatively small Indigenous population compared with other South American countries, due in large part to the Conquest of the Desert campaign in the late 1870s. Argentina's Indigenous people are about 2.4 percent of the population.[1]

Spanish is the national language of Argentina. Other languages are commonly spoken in parts of the country where various immigrant groups settled. Italian is the second-most common language in Argentina with approximately 1.5 million Italian speakers.[2]

Approximately 12,000 people visit the San Telmo Market in Buenos Aires each week to buy food, handmade goods, and more.

Immigration from Syria, Lebanon, and Palestine in the late 1800s and early 1900s resulted in a large number of Arabic speakers in the country. English, German, French, and Welsh are also common European languages in Argentina. More than one million people in Argentina speak Indigenous languages. Quechua is the most widely spoken Indigenous language in Argentina, with more than 800,000 speakers.[3] Other common Indigenous languages are Guaraní and Mapuche.

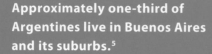

Approximately one-third of Argentines live in Buenos Aires and its suburbs.[5]

In the late 1800s, at a time of increased immigration, a language called Lunfardo was created in Buenos Aires. The language incorporated words from many European languages and some African languages. It began as a pidgin language—a simplified form of communication that immigrants from different nations could use to talk to one another. Lunfardo is still heard today in the lyrics of tango music and in slang terms, especially among young people.

The Argentine Constitution guarantees freedom of religion, and there are small numbers of Jehovah's Witnesses, Mormons, Jews, and people of other faiths, including Indigenous practices. Roman Catholicism, a denomination of Christianity, is the dominant religion in Argentina. Although 92 percent of Argentines identify as Roman Catholic, many no longer practice the faith.[4]

Even though Argentines are less likely to attend weekly services than in the past, Catholicism still plays an important role in Argentine culture. Most people observe Roman Catholic holidays

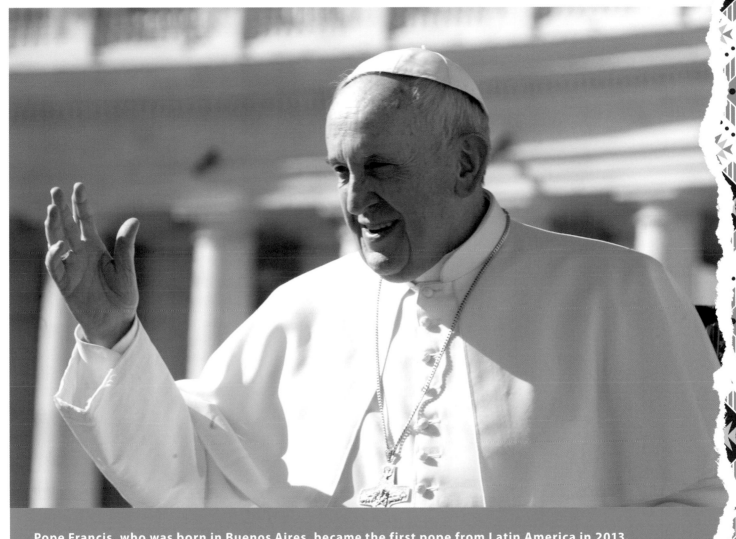

Pope Francis, who was born in Buenos Aires, became the first pope from Latin America in 2013.

such as Christmas and Easter. Lent is an important religious season for Catholics. It is a 40-day period before Easter when Catholics fast and pray. In Argentina, people celebrate a festival called Carnival prior to the Lenten season. Carnival is celebrated with music and dancing in elaborate costumes. Carnival festivals occur throughout Argentina, but many people travel to larger cities to celebrate.

Other major Argentine festivals and celebrations include San Martín Day. This holiday occurs on the third Monday in August. It commemorates the death of José de San Martín, a military leader who helped Argentina gain independence from Spain. Celebrations may last all week with reenactments of military battles, a special church service, and students visiting museums to learn about Argentine history. The week ends with a military band in San Martín Plaza and a moment of silence at 3:00 p.m., the time of San Martín's death.

Venticinco de Mayo, celebrated on May 25, is a national holiday that celebrates the revolution of 1810. A stew, *locro*, made with beef, vegetables,

POPE FRANCIS

Jorge Mario Bergoglio was born in Buenos Aires in 1936. His parents were Italian immigrants. When Bergoglio was 21 years old, he had severe pneumonia, and part of his right lung was removed. He turned to academics, studying humanities and philosophy, and then taught high school while working toward a degree in theology. He became a Roman Catholic priest in 1969. Bergoglio became archbishop of Buenos Aires and later was a cardinal in the Catholic Church. In 2013, Bergoglio was selected to become the pope, the head of the Catholic Church. Priests change their names when they become popes, and Bergoglio became known as Pope Francis. He is the first pope from Latin America.

THE DEVIL FESTIVAL

The celebration of Carnival in the town of Uquía blends Catholicism with Indigenous beliefs. Hundreds of people dress in devil costumes that are decorated with sequins, mirrors, and bells. People wear handmade horns or even real horns from bulls or sheep. In some Indigenous cultures, devils are reborn during the rainy season and signal a growth in vegetation. Carnival occurs in what is late summer or early fall in the Southern Hemisphere. As part of the celebration, people hide behind a sacred hill to thank God and the earth for a good fall harvest.

and dried maize is traditionally served on this day. Argentina celebrates its Independence Day on July 9, the day when the entire country of Argentina declared independence from Spain. Independence Day is celebrated with concerts and fireworks. In addition to national holidays, there are many regional festivals, including the Miracle Festival in Salta in remembrance of an earthquake in 1692, a festival celebrating the founding of Córdoba on July 6, and a wine festival in Mendoza.

THE ARTS

Argentina has a rich history in literature, art, and music. The National Library was founded in Buenos Aires in 1810 and holds more than two million books.[6] There are many museums dedicated to fine art, and some offer classes in art, music, and theater. There are also museums of natural history, ethnology, archaeology, and history.

One of the most well-known Argentine writers is Jorge Luis Borges, who was born in Buenos Aires in 1899. He was a poet, essayist, and short story writer whose works became classics of the 1900s. One of his most famous works is a collection of short stories called *Ficciones*, which was published in 1944.

Argentine artists of the 1900s were heavily influenced by work in Europe and the Americas. Early artists adapted impressionist and cubist styles to Argentina. Later artists were inspired by Mexican murals and pop art from the United States. Antonio Berni, who was born in 1905, was known for creating murals and collages that illustrated the plight of the poor and working class in Argentina.

Other popular artistic mediums in Argentina include theater and film. Quirino Cristiani and Federico Valle produced the first full-length animated film, *El Apóstol*, in 1917. It was political satire about corruption in Buenos Aires. The film was lost when Cristiani's studio burned to the ground in 1926.

Argentina also has a rich musical history. Buenos Aries is known for the Colón Theater, one of the most prestigious opera houses in the world. Opera music was first broadcast on Argentine radio in 1920. The country was the first to have public radio broadcasting. Argentina's musical traditions can be seen in dances. Argentina is particularly known for the tango. Argentine tango has its history in the milonga, a dance originally done by gauchos. The tango is slower than the milonga, more synchronized, and more dramatic. Tango also has influences from Spanish flamenco. Tango became popular in the poor immigrant areas of Buenos Aires in the late 1800s. Today it is performed both on professional stages and in local dance halls. The World Tango Museum is in Buenos Aires.

The iconic tango originated in the Argentine lower classes and has spread throughout the world. Tango's global influence landed it on the UNESCO Lists of Intangible Cultural Heritage.

FOOD

Food in Argentina has a lot of influence from Europe. People often follow the French custom of sweet rolls and coffee for breakfast. Following Spanish tradition, businesses open early and close for a long break at noon, reopening again in the evening. Also in Spanish custom, dinner is served late. Meals often feature Italian dishes such as pasta and pizza.

Alfajores are a dessert made of dulce de leche sandwiched between two cookies.

Beef, usually cooked on a grill, is a major component of the Argentine diet. Raising cattle has been an important part of Argentina's history as well as an economically significant product today. Argentines eat more beef per capita than any country except Uruguay.

Argentines also enjoy dulce de leche, a caramel-like sauce. It is used on ice cream and pastries and can be eaten by itself with a spoon. Argentina and several other countries claim invention of the sweet concoction. The Argentine recipe is unique in adding baking soda. The baking soda helps keep the sauce smooth and creamy.

Another staple of Argentina is yerba maté, a drink similar to green tea and made from the dried leaves of the yerba maté plant, which is native to South America. The Guaraní people introduced the brew to Europeans. Yerba maté contains caffeine. The drink is served in a hollow, round gourd and sipped through a metal straw. Argentines often sit around sharing maté just as Americans might have a coffee break.

Gnocchi—an Italian dumpling made with potatoes and flour—is another important dish in Argentina. Potatoes do not grow well in some areas of Argentina, so yucca is used to make gnocchi instead. Families and friends get together on the twenty-ninth of each month, Gnocchi Day, to eat gnocchi for good luck. The celebration falls at the end of the month, just before payday, because gnocchi is relatively inexpensive to make.

WOMEN'S SOCCER

The women's national soccer team of Argentina has not had the same success and popularity as the men's national team. It scored only two goals in its 2003 and 2007 World Cup appearances while giving up a total of 31 goals.[7] The women's national team did not qualify for the 2015 World Cup and lost all of its funding. The team regrouped in 2017, and the women fought for equality. They received more funding and were able to train in better conditions. However, there is still a long way to go before the teams are treated equally.

SPORTS

Fútbol is the most popular sport in Argentina. In the United States, the sport is known as soccer. Argentina's national team is typically a contender for the FIFA World Cup and won the title in 1978 and 1986. A fierce rivalry exists between soccer teams in Argentina, especially between the River Plate, which is usually supported by the wealthy classes in Buenos Aires, and Boca, whose fans tend to be among the working class.

Argentina has produced soccer stars such as Diego Maradona, who played in the 1980s and 1990s and led the national team to win the 1986 World Cup. Lionel Messi, born in 1987 in Rosario, Argentina, is another famous Argentine soccer player.

Despite its popularity, soccer is not Argentina's national sport. On September 16, 1953, President Juan Perón declared pato the national sport of Argentina. Pato is played by two teams of four horse riders in a large field. The object of the game is for riders to carry a pato ball—a leather ball with stiff leather straps—by its handles and throw it through a vertical hoop to score a goal. Riders hold the ball out by a handle, and opposing players try to grab onto another handle and pull the ball away. The word *pato* means "duck." The game was originally played with a live duck carried in a basket instead of a pato ball. Pato has been played in Argentina since the 1600s. However, the game was banned in the 1800s due to the large number of injuries. The ban was lifted in 1938, and rules were established to make the sport safer. Polo and horse racing are other popular sports in Argentina.

Sports such as tennis, yachting, and power boating are also popular in Argentina. Argentina's geography also offers opportunities for extreme sports. Skiing is popular during the winter in Patagonia. Rock climbers can also challenge themselves to summit peaks in the Andes.

DIEGO MARADONA

Diego Maradona was born in Buenos Aires on October 30, 1960. He is one of the top soccer players of all time. Maradona began his soccer career with the Las Cebollitas soccer club for children at age eight. With Maradona, Las Cebollitas won 136 consecutive games. He joined Argentina's national team at 16, becoming the youngest person to play for the team. Maradona joined Boca Juniors in 1981, helping them win the Argentine Metropolitano championship. He then moved to Europe to play with FC Barcelona in Spain, SSC Napoli in Italy, and Sevilla FC in Spain. He returned to Boca Juniors in 1995 and eventually retired in 1997.

Maradona is best known for Argentina's 1986 World Cup win over England. He scored two goals that were the difference in the game. He scored the first goal with his hand, but the referee did not catch it. It became known as the Hand of God goal. Maradona then dribbled the ball through English defenders and shot past the goalie to score the second goal, often called the Goal of the Century, to give Argentina a 2–1 win. Maradona died of heart problems on November 25, 2020.

Despite his legendary playing career, Maradona had little success as a soccer coach.

CHAPTER SIX

POLITICS

Argentina is a federal republic. Its constitution, which was modeled after the US Constitution, was adopted in 1853. It has been reformed multiple times since its adoption. Like the US government, the Argentine government consists of three branches: the executive branch, the legislative branch, and the judicial branch. The president is the head of the executive branch of government and is also the commander in chief of the military. People vote directly for the president. A presidential candidate must have 45 percent of the vote or 40 percent of the vote plus a ten-percentage-point lead over the second-place candidate to be declared a winner. If no one gets enough votes, a runoff election is held between the first- and second-place candidates.

Construction on the National Congress Building lasted for nearly 50 years.

Alberto Fernández became the president of Argentina in 2019.

The president is responsible for all judicial appointments and is also the chief of the Cabinet of Ministers, a group of people who help the president run the country. An amendment was added to the Argentine Constitution in 1994. Previously, the president was eligible for only a single six-year term. The amendment changed the term length to four years and allowed a president to be elected to two consecutive terms. After two terms in a row, a president must wait one term before being eligible to run again.

The National Congress is the legislative branch of the government. Congress is divided into two houses, called the Senate and the Chamber of Deputies. The Senate has 72 seats. Three senators represent each of Argentina's 23 provinces and the capital district of Buenos Aires. Senators are elected to six-year terms. The Chamber of Deputies has 257 seats. The number of deputies that represent a province depends on the province's population. A province with a large population will have more deputies representing it than a province with a small population. Deputies serve four-year terms.

After the 2019 elections, 42 percent of members of the Chamber of Deputies and 38 percent of the Senate were women.[1]

There are nine Supreme Court judges who are appointed by the president and approved by the Senate. Lower federal judges are first nominated by the Council of Magistrates before being chosen by the president. The Council of Magistrates is part of the judicial branch but includes members from the executive and legislative branches. The first Council was created in 2002. The 13 members of the Council nominate judges, accuse judges of wrongdoing, and depose or suspend judges. Each province has its own system of lower courts.

PARTIES AND VOTING

Argentina has two main political parties. The Justicialist Party is the major liberal party. Its origins are connected to Juan Perón. As a result, members of the party are called Peronists. Most of the supporters of the Justicialist Party are working-class citizens. The Justicialist Party favors more government spending than some of Argentina's other political parties. It was the largest party for almost 40 years until 2021, when it lost its majority in Congress.[2]

The primary challenger of the Justicialist Party is the Radical Civic Union. It is more conservative than the Justicialist Party. The Radical Civic Union has a platform of reforming the judicial system, promoting human rights, and limiting government spending to decrease foreign debt.

Voting is mandatory in Argentina. Citizens must vote in both primary and general elections. Voters who do not register a legitimate excuse for not voting, such as being out of the country, may be fined. Other consequences for failing to vote include losing civil rights, such as being banned from public office for three years. In reality, few people are actually penalized for not voting. In 2012, Argentina passed a new law allowing those aged 16 and 17 to vote. Voting at this age is optional.

INTERNATIONAL AFFAIRS

Argentina is a member of many major global organizations such as the United Nations and the Organization of American States (OAS). The OAS promotes democracy, human rights, security, and

LABOR UNIONS

The Confederación General del Trabajo (CGT) began in 1930 and represented more than 1,100 labor unions in 2022.[3] The CGT won the support of Juan Perón when he was the head of the National Department of Labor. The organization was disbanded after a military coup overthrew Perón when he was president, but it was reestablished in 1985. The CGT's power weakened during times of military rule but resurged under Peronist administrations.

development among its members. It includes all 35 independent countries located in the Americas. Argentina is also a member of the G20, an international organization representing the major economies of the world. The presidency of the G20 rotates between the different countries. Argentina was president of the G20 in 2018 and hosted the first G20 summit in South America.

The country is a regional leader in South America. Along with Brazil, Paraguay, and Uruguay, Argentina is a member of the Southern Common Market, which is also known as Mercosur. The group has successfully expanded trade within the region and is working to expand trade globally.

Argentina has worked with the United States to improve counterterrorism measures. The country is a leading member of the Western Hemisphere Counterterrorism Ministerial and has hosted a conference on counterterrorism

In 2019, Argentine soldiers helped oversee the commemoration of a 1994 terrorist attack in Buenos Aires.

Argentina also helped the United States form the Regional Security Mechanism to counter criminal activity in the Western Hemisphere.

There remains a long-standing feud between Argentina and the United Kingdom over the sovereignty of the Falkland Islands, which Argentina calls the Malvinas Islands. The islands lie 300 miles (482 km) east of the Argentine coast.[4] The United Kingdom has claimed the Falklands since 1771. Argentina proclaimed it owned the Falklands in 1820, leading to conflict between the countries. Tensions reached an all-time high when the Argentine military invaded the Falkland Islands in 1982. The war lasted ten weeks and ended with the defeat of the Argentine military. In 2013, the people of the Falkland Islands voted almost unanimously to remain with the United Kingdom. However, Argentine president Alberto Fernandez is leading the fight to reclaim the waters around the islands.

POLITICAL INSTABILITY

Argentina has not regained the stability and wealth it once had during the peak of Perón's presidency. In 1976, the military seized power after ousting Perón's wife Isabel. The military shut down

TERROR IN ARGENTINA

Argentina has had two major terrorist attacks in recent history. In 1992, an attack on the Israeli embassy killed 29 people.[5] In 1994, the Argentine Israeli Mutual Association, a Jewish cultural center in Buenos Aires, was bombed, resulting in 85 deaths and hundreds of injuries.[6] No one has ever been brought to trial for the attack on the Jewish cultural center. But on the twenty-fifth anniversary of the attack, the Argentine government declared that Hezbollah, an Islamist extremism group, had been responsible.

Relatives of Argentines who had fallen in the Falklands War attended a memorial ceremony in 2009.

Congress, censored the press, and banned trade unions. Fearing Peronist supporters, military forces began a purge of liberal opponents. In what is called the Dirty War (1976–1983), between 10,000 and 30,000 government opponents to the military disappeared or were killed.[7]

The military junta then tried to reestablish democracy. Raúl Alfonsín, a candidate for the Radical Civil Union, won the presidency in 1983. He repealed a law granting amnesty to those involved in the Dirty War and tried to prosecute those involved, including three former presidents under the junta. However, Alfonsín later caved to the military and granted amnesty to some military personnel. This decision, along with hyperinflation, led to riots and eventually Alfonsín's resignation in 1989. He was replaced by President Carlos Menem, who pardoned top officers of the Dirty War. He began an unpopular austerity program—a set of policies that involved increasing taxes and limiting government spending—to try to stabilize the country's economy.

THE DIRTY WAR AND THE UNITED STATES

The United States at times assisted the Argentine government during Argentina's Dirty War. But the US documents about this event had largely been classified until Barack Obama's presidency. In April 2019, the US National Security Council began to declassify information it had collected during Argentina's Dirty War. The documents provided details of human rights violations as well as the names of victims and perpetrators. The US government transferred the declassified documents to Argentina in one of the largest turnovers of such documents in history.

By 1999, the country's massive debt was bringing Argentina to a standstill. The new president, Fernando de la Rúa, unsuccessfully fought rising debt, unemployment, and protests. The economy was failing, and he resigned within a year. In 2001, Argentina's economy collapsed, leading to a default on an international loan from the International Monetary Fund (IMF).

Cristina Fernández de Kirchner, *right*, and her husband, Néstor Kirchner, *left*, celebrate after Fernández de Kirchner won the presidential election in 2007.

In 2003, Néstor Kirchner, a candidate for the Justicialist Party, was elected president and began to stabilize the economy. He negotiated with the IMF to reduce debt, allowing Argentina to pay only the interest on the debt. By 2006, Argentina repaid its multibillion dollar debt to the IMF. Kirchner did not run for a second term.

Kirchner's wife, Cristina Fernández de Kirchner, was elected in 2007. She became the first elected female president of Argentina. With an improving economy, she won a second term in 2011. However, corruption was rife in her administration. Fernández de Kirchner was responsible for giving 16- and 17-year-olds the option to vote. Critics of Fernández de Kirchner accused her of taking advantage of her popularity with young people, as the law added 1.4 million new voters.[8] In 2013, the IMF criticized Argentina for providing false information about economic growth and inflation. Economic problems continued, and in 2014, Argentina defaulted on foreign debt again.

Under the Argentine Constitution, Fernández de Kirchner was not eligible to run for a third term in 2015. She showed strong support for Daniel Scioli. Many feared that Fernández de Kirchner would continue to influence the federal government from behind the scenes if Scioli was elected. However, the conservative opponent, Mauricio Macri, won the 2015 presidential election. His austerity measures were not popular or successful, and the country had to borrow money from the IMF in 2018.

In 2019, inflation was greater than 50 percent.[9] That year, Justicialist Party candidate Alberto Fernández won the presidential election, becoming the first challenger to oust a sitting president. He selected Fernández de Kirchner to be his vice president, a decision that many Argentines viewed as corrupt. After decades of political instability, corruption, and mismanagement, people in Argentina and around the world had low levels of trust in the Argentine government.

> Argentine law requires that 30 percent of candidates from political parties are women.[9]

Protesters gathered outside the National Congress Building in 2018 as lawmakers decided whether Fernández de Kirchner's role in the government granted her immunity against corruption charges.

CHAPTER SEVEN

ECONOMICS

Agriculture and ranching dominated Argentina's economy for much of its history as a nation. Beginning in 1856, more crops were grown in the Pampas region, including wheat, corn and flax. The Argentine government also introduced commercial crops such as sugarcane and cotton and worked to expand its manufacturing industry to bolster the economy from the 1930s to the 1970s. By the mid-1970s, Argentina had become almost self-sufficient in manufactured products as well as fuel.

In 1976, Argentina opened more broadly to the worldwide market. It managed the Argentine peso against foreign currencies, grew government spending, and increased wages. These measures, along with borrowing money to expand manufacturing, resulted

On April 13, 2022, Argentines gathered in the Plaza de Mayo to protest the nation's growing inflation rate.

In May 2022, one US dollar was equal to about 117 Argentine pesos.

in a huge foreign debt. Argentina's national debt caused high inflation rates that drastically devalued the Argentine peso. Argentina issued new money in 1983, with one new peso worth 10,000 old pesos. This peso was replaced with the austral in 1985, but inflation rates continued to climb. In 1989, inflation reached 5,000 percent. From March 1989 to March 1990, inflation grew to 20,000 percent.[1] The country issued another new peso in 1992, which was still in effect in 2022.

In an attempt to control inflation, the Argentine government made the peso equal in value to one US dollar in the 1990s. This meant that the government guaranteed that US dollars in the central bank could be exchanged for an Argentine peso at any time. The government privatized state-owned companies. It could then sell these companies to reduce the national debt. The economy was beginning to grow. But in 1995, economic problems in Mexico affected the confidence of investors in many South American countries. Argentina's economy again began to decline. The recession hit the country hard. Argentina defaulted on foreign debt, and its peso lost value again.

By 2019, Argentina's workforce included millions of employees in different sectors. That year, agriculture accounted for only a small part of the gross domestic product (GDP) because less than 1 percent of Argentines worked in the agricultural sector. Industry, such as manufacturing of goods, employed 22 percent of workers. Most people, 78 percent, worked in services from teaching to tourism.[2]

ENERGY AND NATURAL RESOURCES

Argentina has many energy resources in Patagonia and northwestern Argentina. It has the world's fourth-largest reserve of shale oil and second-largest reserve of shale gas.[3] Energy production increased dramatically in 2022 as the country began to reduce its dependence on foreign oil. Argentine oil refineries process crude oil from Argentina and Venezuela.

Large dams built in western Patagonia produce hydroelectric power. The country has sought to increase production of this renewable energy. Argentina has planned new dams in southern Patagonia. This region has the potential to produce energy from wind too. Argentina is also one of

Environmental activists gathered in Buenos Aires on February 4, 2022. They urged the government to reduce the country's dependence on oil.

Latin America's main producers of nuclear power. In 2022, there were three active nuclear reactors and a fourth being built. Nuclear power provides about 5 percent of the country's electricity.[4]

The country has deposits of iron ore, uranium, lead, zinc, silver, copper, manganese, and tungsten. There is a growing steel industry that supplies steel for its automobile industry. This industry, along with the aircraft industry, has developed quickly due to foreign investment.

TRANSPORTATION AND COMMUNICATION

Today about one-third of Argentina's roads are paved, with most paved roads in urban areas or along trucking routes.[5] More freight is carried by road than railroad in Argentina. In 2022, Argentina joined China's Belt and Road Initiative, a vast network of transportation and energy networks to facilitate trade.

Many rivers in Argentina are too shallow to be navigable. The country has 55 ports but a relatively small shipping fleet.[6] Some ports cater to the tourism industry, bringing tourists into areas such as Puerto Madryn to view wildlife, while others are developed for trade such as the port at Comodoro Rivadavia, which handles shipments of petroleum products. Most large cities have international airports, and smaller towns often have some air service. The country has a national airline, Aerolíneas Argentinas.

There are two telephone companies and three mobile phone companies, which provide good communications throughout the country. Demand for internet service rose during the COVID-19 pandemic. However, 32 percent of households in 2021 did not have fixed internet

service, with a large disparity between regions.[7] Google is building an international submarine cable that will connect the East Coast of the United States with Argentina. This new fiber-optic cable will speed up the process of getting reliable internet service to households in Argentina. China is also increasing its investment in telecommunications in Argentina.

AGRICULTURE

Agriculture accounts for about 7 percent of Argentina's GDP.[8] The large plains of the Pampas are ideal for cattle production. Angus is the major breed of cattle produced. Angus cows are raised almost exclusively for meat, but Argentina also has some dairy cows. In 2020, Argentina was the world's fifth-largest beef exporter.[9] In addition, the agricultural sector grows crops that are used in cattle feed. Patagonia also contributes to Argentina's agricultural sector. It is sheep country, supplying the country's textile manufacturers with wool.

Argentina has approximately 144,800 square miles (375,100 sq km) of agricultural land. Its top export crops are soybeans, corn, wheat, sunflower, barley, and sorghum. Argentina is the

DEFORESTATION IN THE GRAN CHACO

Agriculture and livestock production has expanded into the Gran Chaco. The area faces serious deforestation as trees are cut down to make space for crops and cattle. In the last few decades, 25 percent of the forest has been cleared. An additional 133 square miles (344 sq km) of forest is cleared every month.[10] This has seriously impacted biodiversity, soils, water quality, and climate.

world's third-largest exporter of soybeans, and soybeans account for the largest export revenue of the country.[11] The agricultural sector also produces vegetables and fruits, including citrus fruits, peaches, and plums. Flowers that are cut and sold are part of the agricultural sector. Commercial crops, such as sugarcane and cotton, supply raw materials for the manufacturing sector.

MANUFACTURING

Manufacturing accounts for approximately 29 percent of Argentina's GDP.[12] Nearly 70 percent of the country's exports comes from manufacturing.[13] Food processing—which includes meat processing, cereal production, and beverages—is one of the most important parts of the Argentine economy. Textile production has increased significantly in recent years, boosting the country's clothing industry.

Beyond agricultural processing, the country has an important automobile industry. By value, half of Argentina's imports are machinery and transport equipment.[14] The home appliance and electronics manufacturing industry has grown significantly. Items such as refrigerators, dishwashers, and vacuum cleaners are produced for both domestic use and export.

ARGENTINA'S SPACE INDUSTRY

The Argentina National Space Activities Commission is the country's space program. The commission has launched satellites to observe Earth's oceans and climate. It hopes to use the satellite data for planning in areas such as natural disaster management, health issues, and land use.

SERVICES

The service sector accounts for 64 percent of GDP.[15] This sector includes jobs in banking, retail, transportation, and tourism. Telecommunications and financial services have seen a great deal of growth in recent years due to foreign investment.

Tourism is an important part of Argentina's economy. Most tourists visit from other South American countries as well as from the United States and European countries. Argentina has magnificent landscapes, from the Iguazú Falls in the north to Patagonian glaciers in the south. There are areas of wildlife viewing such as the Patagonian coast.

> More than 300 US companies do business in Argentina, from technology companies to fast-food franchises.[17]

Skiing is popular in winter, and people flock to the beaches in summer. The Las Leñas Resort near Mendoza is famous for skiing and snowboarding on its steep slopes. The Cerro Catedral Resort in western Patagonia is a huge ski resort suited to skiers of all levels. The resort can room more than 7,000 people and has its own mall. Far to the south near Ushuaia is the Cerro Castor Resort, the southernmost ski resort in the world.

Argentina's beaches are also popular destinations. The country has nearly 3,110 miles (5,000 km) of coastline.[16] Beachgoers enjoy white sand beaches and seaside towns. They can paddleboard, enjoy seafood, and go whale watching.

Argentina is a world-class destination for extreme water sports such as white water rafting and kayaking. Mountain trekking and horseback riding are also popular. The more adventurous may enjoy rock climbing and paragliding.

Argentina is also visited for its history and culture. The ruins of Jesuit missions in the north are popular destinations. Buenos Aires is known for its nightlife, museums, monuments, and theaters. In the city, one can learn to tango, shop for elegant products, or visit historic neighborhoods. One of the interesting tourist finds in Buenos Aires is a visit to El Zanjón de Granados. Discovered in the 1980s, the archaeological site is located beneath the San Telmo neighborhood and features an old city. The extensive ruins of old tunnels and rooms may date back to 1536.

CHAPTER EIGHT

ARGENTINA TODAY

Some of the largest problems in Argentina today are high inflation, debt, political instability, and corruption. Argentina has faced low levels of public trust because of these issues. Large-scale shifts in public policy following an election often lead to dysfunction in government, especially in foreign policy. This happened in Argentina with the large swings in the relationship between Argentina and Venezuela. Under Fernández de Kirchner, Argentina built good relations with Venezuela. The Macri administration that followed criticized Venezuela's authoritarian regime, leading to a breakdown

In 2019, corruption in Argentina's judicial department triggered protests. Protesters chanted the slogan *sin justicia, no hay república*, which means "without justice, there is no republic."

in relations. After Alberto Fernández was elected in 2019, Argentina's policies toward Venezuela were once again reversed.

Political corruption is an ongoing problem in Argentina. Transparency International, an organization that fights global corruption, publishes the Corruption Perceptions Index each year. The index rates countries on a scale of zero to 100 based on public perception of corruption. A rating of 100 means there is no perceived corruption. In 2021, Argentina received a rating of 38.[1] Interference in the judiciary was one reason for the low rating. Fernández proposed a major overhaul of the court system that opponents claimed was a way to weaken the Supreme Court. A COVID-19 vaccination scheme gave advantages to those in public office and their friends, further reducing approval from the public.

In recent years, Kirchner and Fernández de Kirchner have been accused of paying as much as $200 million in bribes to government officials during their presidential terms.[2] Fernández de Kirchner was accused of fraud, illicit enrichment, and money laundering. However, she was Fernández's vice president at the time the

> ### PRESIDENT ALBERTO FERNÁNDEZ
>
> Alberto Fernández was born in 1959 in Buenos Aires. He grew up in a wealthy, politically connected family. His grandfather was a senator in La Rioja province, and his father was a federal judge. Fernández got his law degree from the University of Buenos Aires in 1983 and then served in many government positions over the next few decades. His son Estanislao is a drag queen who performs under the name of Dyhzy. Estanislao is a champion for LGBTQ rights.

accusations were made. Argentine law provides immunity for high-authority political figures, and the case was dismissed in 2021.

RESPONSE TO COVID-19

Argentina suffered under the COVID-19 pandemic. The Fernández administration took immediate preparations to detect, isolate, and care for COVID-19 victims. The first case in the country was discovered on March 3, 2020.[3] The government began contact tracing and quarantining those who were exposed to the virus. It closed borders, schools, public spaces, and businesses for two months. It increased the capacities of health-care facilities so that COVID-19 patients would not overwhelm the nation's hospitals. However, the isolation and change of economic and personal routines during the lockdown have shown increased amounts of depression, educational setbacks, and behavioral problems, especially in children.

The economic impact of COVID-19 was significant. Tourism declined and businesses closed. Argentina's economy suffered as the price of petroleum decreased worldwide. In 2020, the country's GDP dropped 9.9 percent.[4]

Fernández tried to take a balanced approach to the economy by encouraging unions to take smaller wage increases, putting price controls on food,

> Argentina had more than 9.3 million confirmed cases of COVID-19 and more than 128,000 deaths through June 2022.[5]

Some crew members aboard the *Ultramarine* cruise ship tested positive for COVID-19 on November 22, 2021. The ship and its members were isolated at Ushuaia Bay for about two weeks until everyone tested negative.

and subsidizing food for the poorest people. Countries control inflation by raising interest rates, and the interest rate from the central bank in Argentina was more than 50 percent in 2022.[6] High inflation not only increases prices for consumers. It also prevents companies from investing in new technology or expansion and discourages foreign investment. The country once more went to the IMF. It got a $44 billion deal in 2022 to avoid defaulting once again on foreign debt.

More than 40 percent of the Argentine population lived in poverty in 2021, with more than 10 percent classed as living in extreme poverty. Poverty especially affects young people. More than half of the people under the age of 14 are poor, and more than 16 percent are extremely poor. Of young people aged 15 to 29, more than 48 percent live in poverty.[7] The middle class shrank during the pandemic as businesses closed and jobs were lost. Poverty rates differ across regions. The rate is highest in the northern part of the country.

Housing has become more of a problem as more people move from rural to urban areas. Poor workers who are unable to find affordable housing live in shantytowns on the outskirts of cities. They build homes of scrap metal or wood and sometimes cardboard. There are often no public utilities.

Despite free education and the country's high literacy rate, Argentina has struggled with dropout rates in both secondary schools and universities. The country is addressing the problem by trying to standardize curriculum and teacher training across the provinces. Teachers' pay is low. Their salaries vary by province, but the average pay for a new teacher is less than the

HYPERINFLATION

Hyperinflation happens when a country's currency loses value over a short period of time. Argentines often deal with an inflation rate of 50 percent each year, one of the highest rates in the world.[8] There have been countries in the past that have dealt with much worse. The highest monthly inflation rate ever recorded was in Hungary in 1946. At the highest point, the monthly inflation rate was 13.6 quadrillion percent.[9]

A 2013 study found that Argentine universities had only a 27 percent graduation rate.[11]

average pay for a bus driver. Strikes in recent years have increased pay but not enough to keep up with inflation.

ENVIRONMENTAL ISSUES

Argentina's major environmental problems are deforestation, loss of agricultural lands, desertification, air pollution, and water pollution. Increasing worldwide demand for food has encouraged large-scale agricultural production in Argentina. This has led to deforestation and habitat destruction in many areas.

Argentina is a country of great biodiversity. Native species account for 98.1 percent of species. However, growth of the agricultural sector threatens many animal species as habitats are destroyed to create farmland. The International Union for Conservation of Nature listed 236 animal species in Argentina as endangered or critically endangered in 2020.[10]

In addition to habitat destruction, deforestation has increased the occurrence of flooding. It also contributes to desertification as fertile soils are washed away and the land becomes less productive. These problems have only worsened because of climate change.

In areas of agricultural production, use of pesticides and herbicides is a serious issue. Chemicals are often applied by airplanes and drift over nearby communities. Studies have found above-average rates of birth defects, cancers, and other health problems associated with high use of pesticides in agricultural areas such as Córdoba.

Although Argentina has many water resources, they are not evenly distributed throughout the country. Even areas with nearby water sources have been seriously affected by pollution. Groundwater in agricultural and industrial areas is often contaminated with heavy metals such as arsenic, mercury, and lead. Consumption of these metals can lead to health problems. Millions of Argentines depend on water from the Matanza-Riachuelo river basin. However, this river system is one of the most polluted in the world. Factories have dumped waste containing heavy metals into the Riachuelo River. Residents in shantytowns near Buenos Aires depend on this river for water for household use.

As an oil-producing country, Argentina contributes greatly to climate change. The country does have significant renewable energy sources such as hydropower and wind power.

In 2021, the waters of the Paraná River dropped to some of the lowest levels in history due to drought.

In 2021, President Fernández promised to limit emissions and increase the nation's renewable energy use from 25 percent to 30 percent by 2030.[12] In addition, he promised to stop illegal deforestation and reduce methane emissions. Methane is a greenhouse gas that is 28 times more damaging than carbon dioxide.[13] It accounts for about 20 percent of global emissions.[14] Humans produce methane through energy generation, rice production, landfills, and raising cattle. Cattle release methane gas as they digest grass. Beef consumption in recent years has fallen because of rising prices caused by ecological concerns and a trend toward healthier eating.

THREATENED PENGUINS

Until the mid-1990s, oil pollution off the coast of Argentina from spills killed about 40,000 penguins a year. The oil industry has cleaned up much of the pollution, but about 1,000 penguins still die from oil each year.[16] Oil pollution damages penguin feathers, affecting the bird's ability to stay warm. Penguins also ingest the toxic oil as they preen their feathers, making them sick. In recent years, the fishing industry has created another threat to penguins. Penguins are accidentally caught in fishing nets and killed.

HUMAN RIGHTS

Argentina passed a law in 2009 that dealt with the prevention of and prosecution for killing women. However, violence against women remains a concern. In 2019, Argentina had 268 cases involving women being murdered and only seven convictions.[15] Reports of domestic and sexual violence increased during the COVID-19 lockdown.

The slums of Buenos Aires, *front*, often lack access to running water and public transportation.

Argentina was the first country in Latin America to legalize same-sex marriage. Since the law was enacted in 2010, more than 20,000 same-sex couples had married by 2020.[17] In 2012, the country passed the Gender Identity Law, which allows people to change their gender and name on their identity card and birth certificate. Fernández decreed in 2020 that at least 1 percent of all federal employees should be transgender.

The Argentine government has marginalized other groups in Argentina. Argentine people believe political influence has led to arbitrary arrests. The number of prisoners increased by 55 percent between 2013 and 2019.[18] With 63,000 people incarcerated, prisons are overcrowded. More than 50 percent of detainees in federal prisons are awaiting trial.[19] In 2020, a council of experts was convened to suggest ways to correct the problem.

Similarly, the Argentine government has harmed Indigenous people. Though the Argentine Constitution protects ownership of traditional lands for Indigenous people, these people face constant encroachment on their lands. Congress passed a law in 2017 that provided for a complete survey of Indigenous lands. In 2020, Argentina returned a total of 1,544 square miles (4,000 sq km) of land to 132 Indigenous communities.[20]

Political instability has marked Argentina since the 1930s. Today, the country continues to struggle with political corruption and a high inflation rate. Argentina is economically connected to other countries in Latin America and is one of the world's leading producers of beef. The country also has a wealth of natural resources such as oil. Its stunning geography and wildlife attract millions of tourists each year. Buenos Aires is a bustling capital city that is a blend of Argentina's history and modern culture. Despite the many challenges Argentina faces, the country remains a regional leader and important member of the global community.

Argentina's national soccer team celebrated with cheering fans after winning a World Cup qualification match against Venezuela in 2022.

ESSENTIAL FACTS

OFFICIAL NAME: ARGENTINE REPUBLIC

GEOGRAPHY

Area: 1,073,518 square miles
(2,780,400 sq km)

Highest Elevation: Mount Aconcagua at
22,841 feet (6,962 m)

Lowest Elevation: Laguna del Carbón at
−344 feet (−105 m)

PEOPLE

Population: 46.2 million (2022 est.)

Most Populous City: Buenos Aires
(15 million)

Ethnic Groups: Mostly European or
mixed European and Indigenous; also
Indigenous, African

Religions: Majority Roman Catholicism,
also Evangelicalism, Jehovah's Witnesses,
the Church of Jesus Christ of Latter-day
Saints, Islam, Judaism

GOVERNMENT

Type of Government:
Presidential republic

Capital: Buenos Aires

Head of State and Government: President

Legislature: Bicameral, with a Senate and
a Chamber of Deputies

ECONOMY

Currency: Argentine peso

Major Industries: Food processing, motor
vehicles, consumer goods, textiles,
chemicals, printing, steel

Natural Resources: Fertile land, lead,
zinc, tin, copper, iron ore, manganese,
petroleum, uranium

NATIONAL SYMBOLS

National Anthem: "Himno Nacional Argentino" ("Argentine National Anthem")

National Bird: Red ovenbird

National Flower: Cockspur coral tree flower

GLOSSARY

AMNESTY

An official pardon granted to people who have been convicted of political offenses or crimes.

AUSTERITY PROGRAM

Measures taken by a government to boost the economy, usually by increasing taxes or making spending cuts in order to pay off debt.

AUTHORITARIAN

Describing a political system that concentrates power in the hands of a leader or small ruling elite and limits civil and political freedoms and rights.

COUP

An attempt to overthrow government leaders.

DEFAULT

To fail to pay or make good on a debt.

DESERTIFICATION

Land degradation, generally caused by human activity.

EXILE

To force a person to leave a country or region for a period of time.

GROSS DOMESTIC PRODUCT (GDP)

The monetary value of all final goods and services produced within a nation's geographic borders over a specified period of time.

INFLATION

An increase in the price of goods and services.

JUNTA

A group that controls a government after a revolution.

MORAINE

Rock and soil deposited at the end or along the side of a glacier.

SOVEREIGNTY

The power of a state or group to govern itself.

STEPPE

An area of flat, treeless grassland.

TREE LINE

The altitude where trees can no longer grow.

ADDITIONAL RESOURCES

SELECTED BIBLIOGRAPHY

"Argentina Geography." *Country Reports*, 2022, countryreports.org. Accessed 1 July 2022.

"History in Argentina." *Frommers*, 2022, frommers.com. Accessed 1 July 2022.

Roy, Diana. "Argentina: A South American Power Struggles for Stability." *Council on Foreign Relations*, 7 Feb. 2022, cfr.org. Accessed 1 July 2022.

FURTHER READINGS

Albiston, Isabel. *Lonely Planet Argentina*. Lonely Planet, 2022.

Hamen, Susan E. *Fighting COVID-19 Abroad*. Abdo, 2023.

Shoup, Kate. *Lionel Messi: Legendary Soccer Player*. Cavendish Square, 2020.

ONLINE RESOURCES

To learn more about Argentina, please visit **abdobooklinks.com** or scan this QR code. These links are routinely monitored and updated to provide the most current information available.

MORE INFORMATION

For more information on this subject, contact or visit the following organizations:

Bernardino Rivadavia Museum of Natural Science
Gallardo, Angel Ave. 490
Buenos Aires, Argentina
turismo.buenosaires.gob.ar/en/otros-establecimientos
/bernardino-rivadavia-natural-science-museum
The Bernardino Rivadavia Museum of Natural Science is one of the most complete
natural history museums in Latin America. It has exhibits on animals, planets, geology,
dinosaurs, and more.

Embassy of the Argentine Republic
1600 New Hampshire Ave. NW
Washington, DC 20009
eeeuu.cancilleria.gob.ar/en
The Embassy of the Argentine Republic in the United States has the answers for
questions about Argentina. It has information about tourism as well as other
information about the country.

SOURCE NOTES

CHAPTER 1. A TOUR OF ARGENTINA

1. "Tourism in Argentina." *WorldData.info*, n.d., worlddata.info. Accessed 15 June 2022.
2. Helmut Sick. "Tinamou." *Encyclopedia Britannica*, 28 Dec. 2017, britannica.com. Accessed 15 June 2022.
3. "Elephant Seals." *National Geographic*, 2022, nationalgeographic.com. Accessed 15 June 2022.
4. "Punta Tombo Magellan Penguin Rookery." *Patagonia-Argentina.com*, 2022, patagonia-argentina.com. Accessed 15 June 2022.

CHAPTER 2. GEOGRAPHY

1. "Argentina." *CIA World Factbook*, 6 June 2022, cia.gov. Accessed 15 June 2022.
2. M. Tulio Velásquez et al. "Andes Mountains." *Encyclopedia Britannica*, 26 May 2022, britannica.com. Accessed 15 June 2022.
3. Robert C. Eidt et al. "Argentina." *Encyclopedia Britannica*, 13 June 2022, britannica.com. Accessed 15 June 2022.
4. Sharon Omondi. "Countries with the Longest Land Borders." *World Atlas*, 1 Aug. 2019, worldatlas.com. Accessed 15 June 2022.
5. "About General Carrera-Buenos Aires." *RList*, n.d., rlist.io. Accessed 15 June 2022.
6. "Los Glaciares National Park." *UNESCO*, 2022, whc.unesco.org. Accessed 15 June 2022.
7. "Argentina Geography." *CountryReports*, 2022, countryreports.org. Accessed 15 June 2022.
8. Eidt et al., "Argentina," *Encyclopedia Britannica*.
9. "Argentina Geography," *CountryReports*.
10. "Iguaçu Falls." *Encyclopedia Britannica*, 5 Sept. 2019, britannica.com. Accessed 15 June 2022.
11. "Argentina Geography," *CountryReports*.
12. Victor Kiprop. "The Largest Lakes in South America." *World Atlas*, 10 July 2018, worldatlas.com. Accessed 15 June 2022.
13. Emilio Fernando Gonzalez Díaz and Kempton E. Webb. "Patagonia." *Encyclopedia Britannica*, 30 July 2021, britannica.com. Accessed 15 June 2022.
14. "The Climate of Patagonia: When to Go to Patagonia." *Travel Guide*, 2020, travelguide-en.org. Accessed 15 June 2022.
15. "Maps of Argentina." *World Atlas*, 24 Feb. 2021, worldatlas.com. Accessed 15 June 2022.
16. John P. Rafferty. "Titanosaurs: 8 of the World's Biggest Dinosaurs." *Encyclopedia Britannica*, n.d., britannica.com. Accessed 15 June 2022.
17. "Southern Cross(ings)." *Rafting Monkey*, 23 Feb. 2018, raftingmonkey.com. Accessed 15 June 2022.
18. Shamseer Mambra. "5 Strait of Magellan Facts You Must Know." *Marine Insight*, 13 Feb. 2021, marineinsight.com. Accessed 15 June 2022.

CHAPTER 3. PLANTS AND ANIMALS

1. "Andean Condor." *National Geographic*, 2022, nationalgeographic.com. Accessed 15 June 2022.

2. Meagan Robidoux. "Pudu puda." *Animal Diversity Web*, 2014, animaldiversity.org. Accessed 15 June 2022.

3. "Capybara." *Encyclopedia Britannica*, 1 Oct. 2021, britannica.com. Accessed 15 June 2022.

4. Cydney Grannan. "What's the Difference between Llamas and Alpacas?" *Encyclopedia Britannica*, n.d., britannica.com. Accessed 15 June 2022.

5. Sheri Dorn and Bodie V. Pennisi. "Pampas Grass." *University of Georgia*, 7 Aug. 2017, extension.uga.edu. Accessed 15 June 2022.

6. "Ombu." *Blue Planet Biomes*, 2002, blueplanetbiomes.org. Accessed 15 June 2022.

7. Sarah Michaels. "Which Mammal Has the Most Teeth?" *World Atlas*, 16 July 2018, worldatlas.com. Accessed 15 June 2022.

8. "Pink Fairy Armadillo Facts." *Fact Animal*, 2022, factanimal.com. Accessed 15 June 2022.

9. "Southern Rockhopper Penguin." *National Geographic*, 2022, nationalgeographic.com. Accessed 15 June 2022.

10. Pablo Teta and Guillermo D'Elía. "Uncovering the Species Diversity of Subterranean Rodents at the End of the World: Three New Species of Patagonian Tuco-Tucos." *National Library of Medicine*, 29 May 2020, ncbi.nlm.nih.gov. Accessed 15 June 2022.

11. "Southern Right Whale." *NOAA Fisheries*, 25 Apr. 2022, fisheries.noaa.gov. Accessed 15 June 2022.

12. Kastalia Medrano. "'Superbird' Cormorant's Deep Dive Caught on Video—A Surprising First." *National Geographic*, 2 Aug. 2012, nationalgeographic.com. Accessed 15 June 2022.

CHAPTER 4. HISTORY

1. Robert C. Eidt et al. "Argentina." *Encyclopedia Britannica*, n.d., britannica.com. Accessed 15 June 2022.

2. Tamar Herzog. "Guaranis and Jesuits." *ReVista*, 29 Mar. 2015, revista.drclas.harvard.edu. Accessed 15 June 2022.

3. Michael T. Luongo. "Argentina Rediscovers Its African Roots." *New York Times*, 12 Sept. 2014, nytimes.com. Accessed 15 June 2022.

4. Luongo, "Argentina Rediscovers Its African Roots," *New York Times*.

5. Eidt et al., "Argentina," *Encyclopedia Britannica*.

6. "Argentina Profile – Timeline." *BBC*, 5 Nov. 2019, bbc.com. Accessed 15 June 2022.

7. Katherine J. Wolfenden. "Perón and the People: Democracy and Authoritarianism in Juan Perón's Argentina." *Inquiries Journal*, 2013, inquiriesjournal.com. Accessed 15 June 2022.

CHAPTER 5. PEOPLE AND CULTURE

1. "Argentina." *CIA World Factbook*, 6 June 2022, cia.gov. Accessed 15 June 2022.
2. Amber Pariona. "What Languages Are Spoken in Argentina?" *World Atlas*, 21 Sept. 2020, worldatlas.com. Accessed 15 June 2022.
3. Pariona, "What Languages Are Spoken in Argentina?" *World Atlas*.
4. "Argentine Culture." *Cultural Atlas*, 2022, culturalatlas.sbs.com.au. Accessed 15 June 2022.
5. Robert C. Eidt et al. "Argentina." *Encyclopedia Britannica*, 13 June 2022, britannica.com. Accessed 15 June 2022.
6. Eidt et al., "Argentina," *Encyclopedia Britannica*.
7. Caroline Chapman. "Women's World Cup: How Argentina Lost Their Team - and Then Fought Back." *BBC*, 19 June 2019, bbc.com. Accessed 15 June 2022.

CHAPTER 6. POLITICS

1. "Argentina." *Freedom House*, 2022, freedomhouse.org. Accessed 15 June 2022.
2. Diana Roy. "Argentina: A South American Power Struggles for Stability." *Council on Foreign Relations*, 7 Feb. 2022, cfr.org. Accessed 15 June 2022.
3. Robert C. Eidt et al. "Argentina." *Encyclopedia Britannica*, n.d., britannica.com. Accessed 15 June 2022.
4. "Falkland Islands War." *Encyclopedia Britannica*, 26 Mar. 2022, britannica.com. Accessed 15 June 2022.
5. Cassandra Garrison. "Argentina Brands Hezbollah Terrorist Organization, Freezes Assets." *Reuters*, 18 July 2019, reuters.com. Accessed 15 June 2022.
6. "Argentina Designates Hezbollah as Terrorist Organization." *BBC*, 18 July 2019, bbc.com. Accessed 15 June 2022.
7. "Dirty War." *Encyclopedia Britannica*, 11 May 2020, britannica.com. Accessed 15 June 2022.
8. "Argentina Lowers the Voting Age to 16." *Americas Quarterly*, 18 Oct. 2012, americasquarterly.org. Accessed 15 June 2022.
9. "Argentina." *World Health Organization*, May 2020, who.int. Accessed 15 June 2022.

CHAPTER 7. ECONOMICS

1. "Case of the Day: Money and Inflation in Argentina." *Reed College*, n.d., reed.edu. Accessed 15 June 2022.
2. Aaron O'Neill. "Argentina: Distribution of Employment by Economic Sector from 2009 to 2019." *Statista*, 16 Feb. 2022, statista.com. Accessed 15 June 2022.
3. "Argentina Oil and Gas." *International Trade Administration*, 29 Oct. 2020, trade.gov. Accessed 15 June 2022.
4. "Nuclear Power in Argentina." *World Nuclear Association*, Aug. 2021, world-nuclear.org. Accessed 15 June 2022.
5. Robert C. Eidt et al. "Argentina." *Encyclopedia Britannica*, n.d., britannica.com. Accessed 15 June 2022.
6. "Argentina." *World Port Source*, n.d., worldportsource.com. Accessed 15 June 2022.
7. "32% of Argentine Households without Fixed Internet Connection, Says Report." *Buenos Aires Times*, 11 June 2021, batimes.com.ar. Accessed 15 June 2022.
8. "Argentina - Economic Sectors." *Nations Encyclopedia*, 2022, nationsencyclopedia.com. Accessed 15 June 2022.
9. Maximilian Heath and Walter Bianchi. "Argentina to Restart Beef Exports to China after Caps Lifted." *Reuters*, 28 Sept. 2021, reuters.com. Accessed 15 June 2022.
10. "Gran Chaco: Protecting the Second-Largest Forest in South America." *Nature Conservancy*, 2022, nature.org. Accessed 15 June 2022.
11. "Agriculture in Argentina: Crops, Productive Areas." *El Sur del Sur*, 2022, surdelsur.com. Accessed 15 June 2022.
12. "Argentina - Economic Sectors," *Nations Encyclopedia*.

13. Joseph Kiprop. "What Are the Biggest Industries in Argentina?" *World Atlas*, 7 Mar. 2018, worldatlas.com. Accessed 15 June 2022.

14. Eidt et al., "Argentina," *Encyclopedia Britannica*.

15. "Argentina - Economic Sectors," *Nations Encyclopedia*.

16. Asif Anwar. "9 Serene Beaches in Argentina Ideal for an Exotic Travel Experience." *Travel Triangle*, 2022, traveltriangle.com. Accessed 15 June 2022.

17. "US Relations with Argentina." *US Department of State*, 9 July 2021, state.gov. Accessed 15 June 2022.

18. "Argentina - Labor Force, Female." *Trading Economics*, June 2022, tradingeconomics.com. Accessed 15 June 2022.

19. "Argentina: Selected Issues." *IMF eLibrary*, 19 Dec. 2017, elibrary.imf.org. Accessed 15 June 2022.

20. Patrick Gillespie. "Argentina's Women Left Behind in Post-Pandemic Jobs Recovery." *Bloomberg*, 31 Aug. 2021, bloomberg.com. Accessed 15 June 2022.

CHAPTER 8. ARGENTINA TODAY

1. "Our Work in Argentina." *Transparency International*, 2022, transparency.org. Accessed 15 June 2022.

2. Josefina Salomón. "Notebooks and Plea Deals: New Weapons against Corruption in Argentina?" *InSight Crime*, 24 Sept. 2018, insightcrime.org. Accessed 15 June 2022.

3. "Argentina." *World Health Organization*, May 2020, who.int. Accessed 15 June 2022.

4. "The World Bank in Argentina." *World Bank*, 13 Apr. 2022, worldbank.org. Accessed 15 June 2022.

5. "Argentina." *Johns Hopkins University & Medicine*, 2022, coronavirus.jhu.edu. Accessed 15 June 2022.

6. Jorge Otaola. "Argentina Interest Rate Seen up 150-350 bps in April after IMF Deal." *Reuters*, 29 Mar. 2022, reuters.com. Accessed 15 June 2022.

7. "Poverty in Argentina Reached 40.6% in First Half of 2021." *Buenos Aires Times*, 1 Oct. 2021, batimes.com.ar. Accessed 15 June 2022.

8. "Inflation Rate by Country 2022." *World Population Review*, 2022, worldpopulationreview.com. Accessed 15 June 2022.

9. Paul Toscano. "The Worst Hyperinflation Situations of All Time." *CNBC*, 29 Jan. 2014, cnbc.com. Accessed 15 June 2022.

10. Valeria Bauni et al. "Biodiversity of Vertebrates in Argentina: Patterns of Richness, Endemism and Conservation Status." *National Library of Medicine*, 4 Feb. 2022, ncbi.nlm.nih.gov. Accessed 15 June 2022.

11. Carlos Monroy. "Education in Argentina." *World Education News + Reviews*, 8 May 2018, wenr.wes.org. Accessed 15 June 2022.

12. "US Relations with Argentina." *US Department of State*, 9 July 2021, state.gov. Accessed 15 June 2022.

13. Amy Quinton. "Cows and Climate Change." *UC Davis*, 27 June 2019, ucdavis.edu. Accessed 15 June 2022.

14. "Importance of Methane." *US Environmental Protection Agency*, 9 June 2022, epa.gov. Accessed 15 June 2022.

15. "Argentina Events of 2020." *Human Rights Watch*, 2022, hrw.org. Accessed 15 June 2022.

16. "Penguins." *Wildlife Conservation Society Argentina*, 2021, argentina.wcs.org. Accessed 15 June 2022.

17. "Argentina Events of 2020," *Human Rights Watch*.

18. "Argentina's Prison Population Grew 55% over Last Six Years." *Buenos Aires Times*, 29 Nov. 2019, batimes.com.ar. Accessed 15 June 2022.

19. "Argentina Events of 2020," *Human Rights Watch*.

20. "Argentina Events of 2020," *Human Rights Watch*.

INDEX

ABOUT THE **AUTHOR**

CYNTHIA KENNEDY HENZEL

Cynthia Kennedy Henzel has a bachelor of science in social studies education and a master of science in geography. She has worked as a teacher-educator in many countries. Currently, she writes fiction and nonfiction books and develops education materials for social studies, history, science, and ELL students. She has written more than 100 books and over 150 stories for young people.